THE CAMELLIA TREASURY

Frontispiece *The desirable landscape camellia Dawn* (C. vernalis) *is used with its own foliage in a small cup holder placed on silver scales—a design for a table.*

THE CAMELLIA TREASURY

For Gardeners, Flower Arrangers and Exhibitors

Mrs. Paul Kincaid

**(All photographs by the author
unless otherwise noted)**

HEARTHSIDE PRESS INCORPORATED

Publishers • *New York*

CONTENTS

To Paul, my husband, who shares my hobbies and allows me to share his. He not only accepts my idiosyncracies but encourages them.

ACKNOWLEDGMENTS

Many people in many places have contributed to this book in various ways. Their warmth and interest have been an inspiration.

Friends from across the seas, who were most gracious and helpful, include: Mr. J. E. Downward, official photographer for the Royal Horticultural Society, Mr. H. G. Hillier, Mr. D. Woodland and Mr. Charles Puddle, all of the United Kingdom; Dr. J. A. Marcellus of Mission City, B. C., Canada; Mr. F. A. Nixon and Mr. R. E. Dean of Hong Kong; Mr. Tom Savige of Australia; and Le Vicomte de Noailles of France.

American friends, who have supplied information and photographs are: Mr. Mark J. Anthony, Descansa Gardens, La Canda, California; Mrs. Jack H. Brown, Greensboro, North Carolina; Mrs. Frank Dowd, Charlotte, North Carolina; Mr. Frank Griffin, Columbia, South Carolina; Mr. Archie Hamil, Goldsboro, North Carolina; Mr. Fred Holder, Bellingrath Gardens, Mobile, Alabama; Mrs. William P. Kemp, Goldsboro, North Carolina; Mrs. Gentry Kidd, Houston, Texas; Mr. Myron Kimnach, Huntington Botanical Gardens, San Marino, California; Mr. Wendell M. Levi, Sumter, South Carolina; Mr. Fred McGee, Florence, South Carolina; Dr. M. R. Mobley, Florence, South Carolina; Mrs. Ralph S. Peer, Los Angeles, California; Mr. R. E. Pittman, Chapel Hill, North Carolina; Mr. Joseph H. Pyron, Executive Secretary and Editor for the American Camellia Society, assisted with pictures and permission to draw on published material. Also, Mrs. Charles Scoggins, Dallas, North Carolina; Mr. Harvey F. Short, La Mesa, California; Mrs. Fisher E. Simmons, Avery Island, Louisiana; Dr. and Mrs. Lee J. Sonnier, Lafayette, Louisiana; Mr. Kenneth M. Sprunt, Orton Plantation, Wilmington, North Carolina; Mrs. Alberta Queen, Gastonia, North Carolina, who typed the manuscript and voluminous correspondence; Dr. Edwin W. Vaughan, Greensboro, North Carolina; Dr. Francis de Vos, United States National Arboretum, Washington, D. C.

Others who have inspired and helped: Mr. Paul A. Von Arnoldi, New York City, and Mr. Leonid Skvirsky, Atlanta, Georgia, photographic artists. Mr. J. Gregory Conway, Fullerton, California; Mrs. Kazuko Ogura of Sapporo, Japan, and New York; and Miss Mary Takahashi of New York City, all leading flower arranging artists and teachers. Mr. Stuart Ortloff, Huntington, New York, landscape architect and author.

My thanks also to my daughter, Kay (Mrs. Fred Moss, Jr.), at whose insistence the book was written, and to my son, Paul Kincaid, Jr., who assisted in many ways.

Mrs. Paul Kincaid

Color Plates

1

CAMELLIAS, PAST, PRESENT, AND FUTURE

Throughout history, men of many nations have looked on the camellia, loved it, and incorporated it into their myths, legends and superstitions. Native to Asia, where the culture of ornamental gardens has been for centuries an integral part of living, the camellia spread throughout the world. At first it was grown outdoors only in warm climates. Later it was widely cultivated under glass. Now—thanks to gardeners who like to try new plants, and to the development of cold-resistant varieties—it is apparent that the camellia has quite a future as an outdoor evergreen tree or shrub in northern climates.

THE NAME AND PRONUNCIATION

In 1735 Carolus Linnaeus, then the world's foremost botanist, named the camellia after George Joseph Kamel, a Jesuit missionary and botanist, using the Latinized version of his name, Camellus. The plant name was pronounced kah-*mell*-yah. More than a hundred years later, Alexandre Dumas' novel, *La Dame*

Aux Camelias, was presented as a play on the English stage, and the title was shortened to *Camille* pronounced Kah-*meel*. From the influence of this play, the plant came to be pronounced kah-*meel*-yah. Most dictionaries, in recognition of common usage, give both pronunciations, but those who know camellia history consider that the original pronounciation should be retained. To the others, kah-*meel*-yah seems natural and familiar.

Whatever the disagreement about pronunciation, it is hard to dispute the statement that the camellia is one of the great gifts of nature to mankind, a double miracle since it blooms in winter when gardens are bare of other flowers.

CAMELLIAS FOR FOOD AND ORNAMENT

The uses of the camellia plant are many and varied. *C. sinensis,* the tea plant which is consumed in Burma, Siam and China as food as well as beverage, belongs to the same family as the garden camellia. In Burma, the leaves of the tea plant are steamed, packed into the ground, and the resulting pickle is served as a delicacy.

In some parts of Japan, young and tender leaves of *C. sasanqua* are steeped for tea which is said to be delicately fragrant and superior in taste to tea made from the leaves of *C. sinensis.* Oils extracted from seeds are used in cooking and for hair grooming; the seeds themselves are dried and made into necklaces, earrings, and finger rings. Wild camellia trees are made into charcoal used for cooking and heating fuel.

Camellia branches are said to make excellent walking sticks because of their strength and flexibility. Leaves are used to make cigarettes and are sometimes dried and made into sachets to be offered at shrines.

THE CAMELLIA IN EUROPE

The journey of the camellia from the Orient to the western world is related to commerce, for it was aboard the spice ships

Plate 1 *The outdoor culture of camellias continues to spread northward. Here they are shown blooming in a foundation planting in a small contemporary garden at Hastings-on-Hudson, New York.* Gottscho-Schleisner photo.

bringing tea, then a sensational new drink, that camellias made their entry in Europe.

Tea achieved immense popularity in Great Britain and prices soared. To capitalize on this, tea merchants ordered living tea plants from China for local cultivation. The Chinese, jealously guarding their monopoly of the industry, are thought to have deliberately substituted ornamental camellias for the desired tea plant. If this was, in fact, the case, then the camellia owes its world-wide distribution to an historical accident produced by a combination of the craftiness of the early merchants and the relationship of the camellia to the tea plant.

Most historians set the date of European introduction at 1739, in which year it is recorded that *C. japonica* from China was grown by Lord Petre in England. Some doubt exists, however, that the British actually were the first to import the camellia. Evidence has been produced that camellias were planted in Oporta, Portugal in the middle of the sixteenth century; whether as garden ornamentals or for use in commerce—for Portuguese mariners were already world famous—cannot be established. We do know, however, that camellias became popular in many parts of Europe, particularly in France, during the nineteenth century. Climate permitting, they were grown outdoors; in colder temperatures, in greenhouses.

THE CAMELLIA ELSEWHERE

The first camellia recorded in the United States was imported from England in 1797 or 1798 by John Stevens, a wealthy resident of Hoboken, New Jersey. This plant was an ordinary wild type, *C. japonica*, bearing single red flowers. In 1800 Michael Foy imported an Alba Plena, a variety still popular and desirable. From 1835 to 1860, camellias were favorite greenhouse plants in the northern part of the United States, and large collections existed in New York, Boston, Philadelphia and Baltimore. Among the early varieties were Alba Plena, Tricolor, Lady Humes Blush and Donckelarii, all of which still rank among the finest grown.

The early history of camellias in the South is sketchy, but it is known that between 1830 and 1860 they had achieved popularity in the seaport towns of the southeast, where they were planted out-of-doors. Many of the plants were purchased from nurseries in the North; others were brought from Europe. Southern planters exported cotton to Europe, and the returning ships brought ornamental plants along with clothing, furniture, china and other household articles.

Camellias reached the West following the Gold Rush. Here too, they were planted outside, in and about San Francisco and Sacramento, during the 1850s. These plants came chiefly from the Atlantic Coast, although some were imported from Europe and others may have been shipped from the Orient.

The first Australian record of camellias imported from Europe dates from 1831. Since then, camellias have become increasingly popular and now are favored garden plants in the southern districts. In fact, Australia and New Zealand are among the most enthusiastic of camellia-growing countries.

CAMELLIAS TODAY

The perfection of form, flower and foliage in the camellia shrub is equaled by no other plant. Although much admired for the flower—it would be an empress even for this one quality—the beauty of the plant in the landscape and its aristocratic behavior with a minimum of maintenance have given it exalted rank with many connoisseurs of the world's flora. There are, and perhaps always will be, a few who are concerned only with the flowers, but most of the dedicated growers feel that the quality of the camellia bloom cannot be measured either by inflated size or newness of variety.

The organization and growth of hundreds of camellia societies here and abroad have widened the horizon of camellia culture. In America, these societies are useful clearinghouses for camellia information. The American Camellia Society, with members in forty states and fifteen foreign countries, serves as a unifying agency for the many societies.

Plate 2   *A segment of the large camellia garden on the estate of Mr. and Mrs. Wendell M. Levi, Sumter, South Carolina near the Atlantic coast. Mr. Levi has done tremendous research and written many reports on the cold-hardiness of camellias.* W. E. Brunson photo.

An International Camellia Society, recently organized, already has members in twenty-one countries, among them Africa, Belgium, China, France, Germany, Greece, Holland, India, Italy, Portugal, Spain, Switzerland, Taiwan and the U.S.S.R. There are members also in America, Australia, Japan, New Zealand and the British Isles.

A few years ago camellia literature was sketchy and sectional; today it is abundant, often national in character. A number of responsible publications have earned positions of authority in America and abroad. Chief among these are the *American Camellia Society Yearbook*; the *Camellia Journal* of the American Camellia Society; and the Southern California Camellia Society's *Camellia Nomenclature*, which is used as a standard for classifying and judging camellias. The Royal Horticultural Society (London) publishes *The Rhododendron and Camellia Yearbook*, and individual societies throughout the camellia-growing districts publish worthwhile, up-to-date literature.

In America, *C. japonica* and *C. sasanqua* are grown out-of-doors in gardens along the Atlantic Coast from Long Island, New York southward into Florida, then westward along the Gulf Coast into Texas. On the Pacific Coast, California deems the camellia a very important garden plant. The camellia is also grown out-of-doors in Washington, Oregon and as far north as Vancouver, B.C.

SPECIES

Today there are more than eighty recognized species of camellias. However, only three are in general use by camellia growers: *C. japonica*, *C. sasanqua* and *C. reticulata*. The vast majority of cultivated camellias—both garden and greenhouse—are japonicas, and references to the camellia always mean *C. japonica*.

C. sasanqua is not as hardy, nor are its blooms as large, enduring or spectacular as those of *C. japonica;* but the plant fulfills many landscape needs and its blooms provide lovely fall color. Although most varieties shatter very quickly, while they last, they are charming in flower arrangements.

C. reticulata produces some of the finest of all camellia blooms, but the plant is sparse, lanky, sensitive to cold, and hard to grow. It is therefore found chiefly in greenhouse collections. Only a few other species are used as garden plants: *C. cuspidata, C. hiemalis, C. maliflora, C. saluenensis, C. sinensis* and *C. vernalis.*

A good deal of interest has been centered in recent years on the Snow camellia, *C. rusticana,* because of the possibilities for hybridizing it for cold hardiness.

There is also wide interest in *C. granthamiana,* the most recent introduction. Not closely related to any other known species, it bears handsome, waxy, white flowers, five and one-half inches in diameter, formed by eight petals around a cluster of golden stamens, with interesting, leathery foliage. Although only one plant has been found, on a remote slope of Tai-mo Shan, Hong Kong, 2000 feet above sea level, this species is easy to grow from cuttings. A number of small plants obtained in this manner have been distributed to nurseries and to collectors.

Plant breeding is a lengthy task; several generations must be bred before the best qualities of two or more species can be considered stable. *C. japonica, C. sasanqua* and *C. reticulata* had been under cultivation in the Orient for hundreds of years before they were brought to western gardens.

The possibilities in many of the species are still to be entirely explored. It is fun to dream what the next few generations will bring; it is sensible also to appreciate many of the camellias already here.

THE FUTURE OF CAMELLIAS

We are entering a new and exciting age in camellia cultivation. Modern genetics and the discovery of species hitherto unknown have stimulated the hybridizer and opened new doors to him. One of these doors may give access to northern Indochina where camellias are known to exist with yellow, purple and coral blooms! The introduction of a true yellow would enable hybrid-izers to produce the same color combinations in camellias that are found in roses. The areas in which camellias can be success-fully grown will be considerably extended in future years by breeding for hardiness and by adapting certain varieties to colder climates.

Camellia japonica no doubt will hold its first place in the camellia world, but there will be continued advancement in old varieties, superior new varieties and interspecific hybrids.

As camellia societies grow on an international level, and as camellia lovers throughout the world draw closer, hitherto unknown sources of information, relevant to the history, the nomenclature and the future of the camellias, will be brought to light.

Plate 3 *Large camellia plants under moss-hung live oaks form an elegant setting for this lovely formal garden. To achieve a dense background mass, camellias can be planted four to six feet apart. Some authorities recommend planting ten to twelve feet apart, which is good for a very long-range plan, but most of us don't want to wait too many years to reach our goal. Bellingrath Gardens.*

2

𝒥N THE LANDSCAPE

Camellia growers can be divided into three groups. The first group is composed of the collector or hobbyist who aims only to produce outstanding, new and novel blossoms. He is too busy looking for "collector's items," counting buds and dreaming of bigger and better flowers, to enjoy the scenery. The overall beauty of his grounds does not concern him; every available inch of his garden is planted to camellias, with new varieties and irresistible buys overflowing the lawn.

In the second group is the average gardener. Enamored of the elegance of the plant when seen in its glory—few can resist this magnificent shrub with its many flower forms and colors —he buys impulsively, wanting many different varieties of gorgeous blooms. Such a buyer is unlikely to use the camellia to its best advantage, unless his design sense is so instinctive that he plans as he plants—design by accident, so to speak.

In the third group is the gardener who sees in the camellia a material of the appropriate texture, shape and hue to achieve a design purpose in the landscape. His interest is in selecting a plant, not for its moment of bloom, but for its year-round dependability. If he is a practical designer, he will also select material which requires minimum care.

Whatever the impetus for his purchase, each type of buyer discovers that the camellia is "blest with charm, that certainty to please." So it has always been for me. The lovely camellia has never failed to please, whether I am counting its buds or enjoying its quiet beauty from my kitchen window. (Color Plate IV.)

DESIGNING THE GARDEN

The landscape designer views plants in perspective, as a part of the visible scene. He sees them as media for creating living pictures, changing with the seasons but always lovely and interesting. Although we in the United States specialize in specialization, it is unfortunate that few new home owners engage a landscape architect to design the gardens which represent so large a part of their total investment in real estate.

Of course, by studying the literature on the subject, it is possible for the interested gardener to plan a place that is esthetically suited to the house, with open areas to give a sense of space, enclosed sections for privacy, and concealed areas for utility. Many excellent books are on the market; one of the best is *Garden Design* by Sylvia Crowe (Hearthside Press, Inc.). In addition, the National Council of State Garden Clubs, Inc., cooperating with many state universities, offers its members streamlined courses in landscape design.

Anyone with even the slightest knowledge of art theory, whether expressed in music, painting, literature or other media, will recognize at least some of the following references to basic design principles. Dominance or unity, rhythm, balance, focalization, contrast, scale, proportion, and repetition; these words, or their synonyms, sum up the qualities which define all art. In the chapter entitled "The ABC's of Design" I have explained these principles in relation to flowers arranged in containers; however, the explanation is as directly applicable to plants arranged in the garden.

FRAMEWORK OR FOCAL POINT?

The camellia may be planted individually for focalization and accent. It has the virtue, which every specimen needs, of great style and form; it also is easily maintained and attractive at all times. Planted for mass effect, the plants acquire homogeneity, their lines merging into one another so that the effect is of a sea of dark green. Against this mass of green, any kind of flower sparkles like a jewel in its setting.

THE SMALL CONTEMPORARY GARDEN

As home grounds have diminished in size, due primarily to increased cost of land and materials, high taxes, and scarcity of efficient garden help, the camellia has become increasingly popular. Today, in many parts of the world, it is regarded as one of the finest of outdoor evergreen and flowering plants. The old idea that camellias are expensive, hard to maintain, difficult to grow, and limited in use, has been proved false.

Certainly, the camellia is versatile. With it, one can as effectively create the feeling of a formal classical garden as of the casual woodland glade. It is as appropriate for the small suburban plot as for the large country estate. The success of the plant in varied situations is due to its perfect proportions and the ease with which its size may be controlled in relation to its surroundings. Camellias tolerate very heavy pruning.

The small garden should rely chiefly on japonicas, although a few good sasanquas will give the variety and emphasis which every design needs.

THE CAMELLIA IN THE PERIOD GARDEN

The camellia traveled world-wide from the Far East, so not surprisingly it seems at home in many different styles of gardens. In Plate 8, for example, it is oriented to a setting that could have had its inspiration in Spain, complete with lovely arches, handsome ironwork and patterned tiles. Plate 7 evokes for me the richness of the Italian garden with its emphasis on foliage rather than flower, with its terraces, steps, plants in containers, and water to reinforce the comparison. In Color Plate IV with its broad curves and sweeping movement reminiscent of a naturalistic English garden, camellias are shown grouped for mass effect.

CAMELLIAS FOR ACCENT

By choosing camellias that are normally upright in habit, and by tip pruning these until they fit the desired appearance, attractive accent plants may be developed for use in the garden or along walls or fences. In a small garden where space is limited, upright growers can be planted closely; thus, a larger number of plants may be used than would be possible otherwise. For contrast, a columnar plant may be placed between two bushy plants with a low, slow-growing variety, bold in color, placed in the foreground.

Some suggested varieties for columnar, pillar or pyramid forms are Eleanor Hagood, Elena Nobile, Kumasaka, Mrs. Lyman Clarke, Marjorie Magnificent, Pink Ball; Royal Trumpeteer and Showa-Supreme (*C. hiemalis*), and Apple Blossom (*C. sasanqua*).

While it is possible, through selective pruning, to tailor any variety into almost any desired shape, it is best to take advantage of natural characteristics and select according to your design needs.

Plate 4 *A vista in the garden of Mr. and Mrs. William P. Kemp, Goldsboro, North Carolina, is bounded by a serpentine wall which defines a handsome sculptured figure. The sunken patio with its bubbling fountain creates a pleasant oasis; the benches invite quiet enjoyment. Camellias are the dominant plants, but companions which enjoy the same conditions of shade, moisture, and acid soil are included. This scene shows ivy, boxwood, Japanese yew, dogwood and bulbs. Ball Studio photo.*

HEDGES

A camellia hedge is a thing of beauty twelve months of the year, but it is breath-taking in bloom. The plants may be clipped in formal style, but are more graceful when allowed to grow loosely and informally, shaped only by judicious pruning. A camellia hedge should never be sheared hard like privet, but should be carefully shaped to the desired form over the years. Dwarf types should be planted about three feet apart, taller ones four feet apart.

It is more effective to use only one variety, except when the hedge is long, in which case one plant or group of plants of a different variety, perhaps bolder in color, may be added for accent.

The variety or varieties recommended for a hedge will depend on the height desired. For a low hedge, choose low growers such as Tanya (*C. sasanqua*) and Shishi-Gashira (*C. hiemalis*). For a medium hedge Covina is outstanding. For a tall hedge, Prof. Charles S. Sargent and Cleopatra (*C. sasanqua*) are often used, but many other fast, upright growers are equally good.

ESPALIERS

"Espalier" is derived from the French word for shoulder; it denotes training the branches, or arms, at right angles to the trunk or body. Two types are popular; one, the *Palmetto*, forms a flat, fan-shaped pattern; the other, the *Candelabra*, is trained to a single leader and branched in equidistant parallel lines. As an espaliered plant matures, it becomes quite a conversation piece. Certainly in the small garden it produces maximum design for minimum space.

Many garden settings are lovely for espaliers. I visualize them along walls or fences, possibly in contrast with a plant trained as a tree standard or pillar, near a walk where space is limited, against the blank wall of a house or right-angled garage, on a protruding chimney, or at the side of a patio as a center of interest. It can be trained on a trellis in the open, or on a lattice against a wall.

Plate 5 *Another view of the Kemp garden shows a camellia hedge, growing informally, with masses of azaleas in full bloom, dogwoods and towering pines. Now one of the most charming gardens I have ever visited, the site was once a city dump! Later, it became a country club golf course, which in some ways offered an even greater challenge, since a sense of seclusion and intimacy had to be created if the garden was to be successful for its then new owners.* Ball Studio photo.

Plate 6 *How pleasant for an altar committee in charge of flowers to have a garden like this for discreet cutting! Camellias espaliered against brick walls, a delightful lead statue of St. Francis of Assisi, and a fountain are located in the garth of St. Steven's Episcopal Church in Goldsboro, North Carolina.* Ball Studio photo.

Among the numerous varieties that lend themselves well to espalier are Alba Plena, Berenice Boddy, C. M. Wilson, Coral Pink Lotus, Coronation, Elegans, Gigantea, Harlequin, Magnoliaeflora (charming, but a slow grower), Masterpiece and Mathotiana.

Sasanquas are exquisite used as espaliers, for example, Mineno-yuki and Hugh Evans. Dawn (*C. vernalis*) and Showa-No-Sakae (*C. hiemalis*) are also desirable. Local nurserymen can make other suggestions.

STANDARDS

Tree or standard forms add variety and interest to a garden. A pair of standards planted on either side of a gate or on a patio can be very striking. Planted in containers, they can be moved from place to place to create interesting effects, but be sure their color adds to the landscape harmony and is not in conflict with it.

Most camellias become trees after many years. A camellia standard, like a rose standard, is made by pruning and training a young plant to look like a small tree.

Two methods of making standards are used. The simpler is to choose a straight-stemmed, bushy specimen, five or six feet tall, and cut away all branches to a height of three or four feet. Prune the remaining branches at the top to form a rounded head. The plant will be top-heavy and need to be staked. Prune carefully every year. Almost any straight-stemmed, compact-growing camellia is suitable for this style: Debutante, Finlandia, Pink Perfection and Reg Ragland to name a few.

The other method is to use a plant with a tall, straight trunk and graft it at a considerable distance above the ground. Beautiful effects can be achieved by grafting weeping or trailing varieties to the standard. Two or four scions should be used, depending on the size of the understock. Showa-No-Sakae (*C. hiemalis*) is exceptionally well-suited for this style.

Standards may be grown in the ground, in elegant Italian or other pottery urns, or in good-looking redwood tubs. Since containers are portable, they may be moved to vantage points in garden or patio..

TRELLISES

The training of plants of naturally vining character onto or over trellises, as climbing roses are trained, can be a novelty. Consider a shady garden path, overhung with trellised camellias, complemented by small azaleas massed on each side. Varieties that lend themselves perfectly for such displays are Hit Parade, Singing Fountain, Bride's Bouquet, Setsugekka (*C. sasanqua*) and Showa-No-Sakae (*C. hiemalis*).

GROUND COVERS AND EDGING

Camellias of slow growth and willowy or sprawling habit are charming planted as an edging in front of beds of larger camellias, or planted as a ground cover along garden paths and shady banks. So used, they should be spaced about three feet apart. Encourage them to grow horizontally by topping to produce side growth, and by carefully spreading and tying branches at intervals several inches above the ground. Some camellias that are effective in this way are Elegans and its sports, and the sasanquas Mino-no-yuki, Pink Snow and Tanya. The *C. hiemalis* Showa-No-Sakae and Shishi-Gashira are also excellent.

CAMELLIA COMPANIONS

Many camellia devotees carry their enthusiasm for this particular plant to the point of excluding most others. This is unfortunate because the camellia garden is lovelier and more interesting with companions to bring variety or pleasing repetition of texture, color and form. In my garden, companion plants are chosen not only to enhance the scenery, but also to provide material for flower arrangements. A sound basis for successful flower arrangement is to be an enthusiastic gardener with a love for plants bearing unusually beautiful flowers, foliage and fruit. To the arranger, the camellia garden can be a vast palette the whole year. Succession of bloom can be attained through intelligent choice of plants. In selecting companions, apply a principle of Japanese design and combine vertical, recumbent and horizontal shapes for the sake of variety.

Plate 7 *Reminiscent of the Spanish Steps in Rome is this scene from Bellingrath Gardens, with flowing water to reinforce the comparison to an Italian garden. Towering trees are underplanted with large camellias, their dark green foliage making a magnificent background for the blaze of azaleas in containers on the stone steps and clustered at the base of the waterfall.*

Because camellia areas are widely separated, and ever-expanding, the list of plants that could thrive with them is almost unlimited. The camellia does not like lime-sweet or dry soil, but is otherwise most agreeable and tolerant. Therefore, every gardener should study conditions in his own garden. These, and his personal taste, will be deciding factors in selecting plant neighbors for the lovely camellia.

The camellia garden need never be a dull or monotonous horticultural display. If well-designed, an all-green garden, like an all-green flower arrangement, is a joy to behold even when it is out of season, that is, when camellias are not in bloom.

WITH OTHER SHRUBS

Probably the companion most planted in camellia gardens is the azalea. Easy to grow, and with a marked preference for acid soil, its fine foliage contrasts well with the heavier foliage of the camellia. Winter bronzing in some of the evergreen varieties adds to their value. One caution, however: their color range is wide and brilliant varieties may clash with bright camellias. Do not plant haphazardly or you may get such discords as orange azaleas with shell pink camellias. A good, simple rule to follow is to use blue-reds and blue-pinks together, yellow-reds and coral tones together, and lots of white and cream colors as peacemakers between groups.

Other shrubs which do well in the camellia garden are hollies in infinite variety, their small, fine leaves making a strong textural contrast for camellias; the spiny-leaved mahonia; fern-like nandina; pittosporum (its dark leaves offering good contrast for shiny camellia foliage); cherry laurel (*Prunus caroliniana*) for its light green foliage; illicium; andromeda; myrtle (*Myrtus communis*); gardenia; oleander (*Nerium Oleander*); sweet olive (*Osmanthus fragrans*); cleyera japonica; photinia (both *P. serrulata* and *P. glabra*), and many varieties of viburnum. Euonymus, with its leather-like dark leaves; hybrid rhododendron (which in our climate never loses its good appearance;

I. *Camellias flourish in the shade of pine trees, the needles providing the perfect mulch for acid-loving, woodland plants. This scene is from the Camellia Arboretum, Bellingrath Gardens.*

II. *Wind and waves fashioned the gray branch, which fits easily into a tall black pottery container, requiring no special mechanics. The white marble base is from old store scales. One white Elizabeth Boardman camellia and one red Blood of China complete the design.*

further north its leaves curl under in cold weather); various forms of box; pyracantha; ligustrum; banana-shrub (*Michelia fuscata*); loquat; *Kalmia latifolia;* hemlock (*Tsuga canadensis*); cotoneaster; the graceful abelia; podocarpus; *Pieris japonica,* for its exquisite cupped, pale pink flower and handsome foliage; *Kerria japonica;* leucothoe; acuba; winter Jasmine; cunninghamia, and yucca are all useful. The fragrance of *Elaeagnus pungens* and *Daphne odora* contribute the one quality missing in the camellia—fragrance. Groups of wintersweet, flowering quince and many other deciduous early flowering shrubs placed inconspicuously in the background, provide good line material for arrangements.

BORDERS AND GROUND COVERS

Hosta, in many species and forms, *Arum itallicum* and aspidistra thrive in the camellia border and provide wonderful foliage. Excellent plants for facing down the beds and borders and for ground covers are liriope, muscari and several varieties of ophiopogon, dwarf gardenias, dwarf late-flowering Satsuki and Chugai azaleas, epimedium, ajuga, vinca minor and pachysandra.

Most of my borders are edged with liriope. It is attractive the year around, prevents washing, and keeps the lawn grass from creeping into the borders.

VINES

Vines good in the camellia bed are ivy, climbing varieties of euonymus, star jasmine (*Trachelospermum jasminoides*), and wisteria. Climbing roses are lovely and will tolerate some shade. Rose plants do not really have good form, a condition which is concealed from the beholder if planted with camellias. Where climate permits, the brilliant bougainvillea makes a colorful companion for camellias.

COMPANION TREES

Trees of various kinds furnish a valuable high canopy, giving shade, accent, screening and background; and creating the effect of woods, so natural for camellias. Pines and oaks are two of the best, the finely textured pine needles, picturesque oak and glossy camellia leaves making a well-scaled harmony of textures. I am fortunate to have found the oak and pine growing naturally to back my camellia planting. Bamboo, willow and ginko are also good. Flowering trees increase year-round beauty and interest, and add considerably to the garden scene. Few trees can rival the splendid flowering dogwood (*Cornus florida*), and the redbud (*Cercis canadensis*) with its purplish pink flowers and the rarer white form. The spectacular fruit trees—crab apple, cherry, peach, plum, etc., and early flowering magnolias (*M. stellata, M. soulangeana, M. liliflora,* etc.)—are effective blooming with bulbs against a background of late camellias. Branches from flowering trees and shrubs may be forced into bloom indoors to give height to camellia arrangements from mid-winter to spring. Crepe myrtle (*Lagerstroemia indica*), witch-hazel (*Hamamelis virginiana*), the camellia-like *Frankliana Alatamaha* and the narrow cryptomeria—which also comes from Japan—are effective in warm zones. Palms in many varieties are irresistible to gardeners who have moved from a cold climate to areas where they can be grown.

BULBS AND WILDLINGS

I love snowdrops, crocus, scillas, hyacinths, anemone, mertensia, bleeding heart (*Dicentra spectabilis*) and many more small bulbs which add variety and interest and augment early spring bloom. Later, daffodils and tulips are charming. The dark green camellia plants, usually through blooming, are a perfect background for the bright bulbs.

Ours is a woodland garden and wild flowers and camellias are exceptionally compatible. Ferns are particularly graceful in the summer camellia garden. Caladium, coleus and other foliage plants add varied textures and colors. Lilies, daylilies (in the sunnier spots), begonias (all kinds, including tuberous

Plate 8 *This patio of the Bellingrath home in Theodore, Alabama has the look of a Spanish courtyard, richness of architecture, use of ironwork, and a fountain as a focal point being typical of Hispano-Moorish design. Sasanquas provide a lovely border, the solidity of the plants and their growth to ground level recommending their use for the purpose. Plants in containers are changed as their season of bloom ends.*

ones), fuchsias, primroses and clivias add a note of color at various times. Many annuals and perennials will thrive in the camellia garden, but in the summer, when sitting in the shade has more appeal than working and weeding annuals, I enjoy an all-green garden. Not widely used, but most effective, are the fall flowering bulbs. I have tried lycoris (*L. radiata*) with its red, spider-like flowers; sternbergia (*S. lutea*); colchicum, and autumn-flowering crocus, planted satisfyingly in clumps and drifts.

Whatever your choice of plants, dig in the garden and leave anger, tears and frustration buried there. Work with nature and be in larger kinship with God. Then, no matter how small the role, you are playing a real part in God's design for the world.

3

CHOOSING CAMELLIAS: A PERSONAL APPROACH

The camellia exerts such a charm and fascination over most of us that it is hard to approach the choice of varieties with common sense. In my garden, the fine old, standard varieties prevail over the newcomers, because it is difficult to estimate the intrinsic value of a camellia until it has been grown under varied conditions and for a number of years. Old-timers consistently win prizes in competition with newer varieties for good reason—most of them are better.

For a well-rounded collection, if climate permits select varieties that provide succession of bloom from early fall through late spring. If selections span the entire blooming season, there are bound to be blooms untouched by bad weather.

There are camellias in both growth habit and flower composition to meet any requirement for garden or vase arrangement—low, squatty varieties; tall, open growers; broad, willowy varieties; dense, full plants; tall, columnar forms. The flowers are from two to six or more inches across.

COLOR RANGE

The color range is wide, from pure white to creamy white, from salmon pink to scarlet, from clear pink through various shades of rose to black-red; there are many, many variegated flowers, too. I like to keep together the orchid and lavender pinks, clear pinks with accents of red, yellow-reds and corals, with white and cream plants used as buffers between color groups. I save the boldest colors for strong contrast in the foreground when growth habit permits.

BUYING CAMELLIAS

Before buying camellias, have a plan for their use and know the forms and colors you like. A large collection is not necessary; a few carefully selected, healthy ones will yield flowers for arrangements, corsages and garden bloom over a long period.

Buy only as many plants as you can easily care for. There is little enjoyment if the camellia garden becomes a chore to maintain. It is far better to have a few healthy, well-groomed and attractively placed varieties than many neglected, imprudently chosen and carelessly arranged ones.

The hundreds of varieties from which to choose—many so near alike that they are distinguishable only by a few of the experts—and the unreliability of nomenclature bewilder the beginner.

The same varieties grown under different climatic and cultural conditions do not always perform in the same way. Names of camellias in different countries and sections do not always agree. Often, camellias sent from one country to another are differently named. Sometimes, even in the same area nurseries give different names to the same variety. It is not uncommon to buy one variety over and over, sold under different names by different growers.

New growers should go to camellia shows, scan catalogues, visit nurseries at blooming time and inspect test gardens as well as public and private camellia gardens. People are delighted to show their gardens in bloom. Join the local and national camellia societies. Make lists as you learn and observe; discuss the lists with growers in the same area.

FOR NORTHERN GARDENS

Buy only from reputable nurserymen and, if possible, from one nearby who is a camellia specialist. Camellias for northern gardens should be purchased from the most northerly source possible: these plants will be acclimated to the region. However, if your nurseryman cannot meet your needs, do not hesitate to order from distant reputable nurseries. Good nurseries can properly pack plants and guarantee delivery in good condition many hundreds of miles away.

In selecting plants from local sources, look for a good green, crisp color and a general appearance of vigor. Do not choose plants with yellow leaves, dead wood or blemished bark. Avoid the temptation of buying a sickly plant full of buds instead of a healthy plant with few or no buds. Generally, the small plant with many buds is a sick plant.

IN CAN, B & B OR BAREFOOT?

It is safe to buy plants either balled-and-burlapped (B&B) or in cans. The latter can be bought at any time of the year and planted later. They will also have all their roots. On the other hand, if you want a large plant, almost always it will be B & B. It is important to ascertain that it has been root-pruned. Very large plants can be moved with safety if they have been root-pruned, but even a small one may be lost if it has not. This problem is one against which a reliable dealer will protect you.

Unless the variety preferred is a weak grower, or is a new variety which you want quickly, there is no reason to buy a more expensive grafted plant.

Plants are also bought bareroot. If they have been carefully dug and prepared for shipment, planted immediately upon receipt, and kept well-watered, they will present no problems.

Plate 9   *Semi-double Alba Superba camellias and camellia foliage with driftwood, arranged for one of my lecture-demonstrations. This is a recommended variety for the garden of a flower arranger.*

BLOOM FORMS

There are so many combinations of floral characteristics that it is almost impossible to restrict all camellia blooms to the six recognized categories. Often a single plant will bloom with more than one form. The classification of flower formations of varieties of *Camellia japonica* is as follows:

1. *Single.* Not more than eight petals in America. Not more than nine petals in Great Britain.
2. *Semi-double.* Two or more rows of petals. Conspicuous stamens in most varieties.
3. *Anemone Form.* One or more rows of outer petals lying flat, the center a convex mass composed of petaloids and stamens.
4. *Peony Form.* A deep, rounded flower with loose petals and stamens intermingled, to a convex mass of petals, petaloids and stamens, or massed irregular petals never showing stamens.
5. *Rose Form Double.* Imbricated petals showing stamens in a concave center when fully open.
6. *Formal Double.* Fully imbricated, many rows of petals, no visible stamens.

RECOMMENDED VARIETIES

A list of varieties chosen from the hundreds of those available can never be complete or suitable for all districts. The plants listed below have grown satisfactorily in my garden over a number of years, many for as long as twenty-five years. This garden is not in the coldest camellia-growing region; neither is it in a camellia belt. Until a few years ago, a camellia in this Piedmont section was considered a curiosity. The natural tendency of gardeners to experiment with plant varieties that are not native to their climate has been the source of many wonderful discoveries. I am a pioneer in growing and promoting camellias in an area outside the traditional camellia belt. Today camellias are grown outdoors as far north as Long Island, New York. It has been established that varieties of camellias are dissimilar in hardiness and some plants are tolerant of very low temperatures ($-15°$ F). The flowers are less tolerant, but northern gardeners report enjoying camellia blooms at least four years out of five.

In my garden, there has never been a year when I did not have some camellia blooms; only twice in twenty-five years has there been a severe loss of buds. All plants have withstood a low of 2° F and a high of 106° F. The following list, therefore, represents a good cross section.

Code
*—Especially recommended for
   both garden and flower arranging
E—Early
M—Midseason
L—Late

WHITE CAMELLIAS

ALBA PLENA
> Formal Double. Large bloom. Slow, bushy growth. Medium-size flowers excellent for corsages. The second to reach America and still a great favorite. Flowers easily browned by cold.   E—M

*ALBA SUPERBA
> Semi-double. Medium-size bloom. Upright growth. Hardy. M—L

*DELECTISSIMA
> Single. Medium-size bloom, often with a pink stripe. Excellent spreading growth. Charming for flower arranging. E—M

*DUCHESS OF SUTHERLAND
> Semi-double. Large bloom, often with a pink stripe on one petal. Upright growth.   M—L

*ELIZABETH BOARDMAN
> Semi-double. Very large bloom with fluted petals. Bushy, upright growth. One of the best white camellias.   M

EMMETT BARNES
> Semi-double. Large bloom with deep, ruffled petals. Compact growth.   E

*FINLANDIA
Semi-double. Large bloom with swirled and fluted petals. Vigorous compact growth. One of the best. Exceptionally fine for all uses. Other good forms of this variety include Finlandia Blush, Finlandia Red, Finlandia var., King Lear (red marbled white), Monte Carlo (pink), Alice Morrison (pink). E–M

*FLORENCE STRATTON
Formal to Rose Form Double with cupped inner petals. Medium to large bloom. Some petals solid pink. Vigorous, bushy growth with excellent foliage. L

FRIZZLE WHITE (Susan Carter)
Semi-double. Large bloom with wavy, crinkled petals. Spreading growth. M

GEORGE BARRETT
Semi-double with large, fluted outer petals to Peony Form bloom. Compact growth. E–M

*HAKU-RAKUTEN
Semi-double to Peony Form with fluted petals. Large bloom. Upright growth. Cold hardy. M–L

JOSHUA E. YOUTZ (White Diakagura)
Peony Form to Formal Double. Large. Slow, compact growth. Exceptionally beautiful bloom but sometimes temperamental. I use it often at Christmas with Madonnas. E

K. SAWADA
Formal to Rose Form Double. Large. Vigorous bushy growth. Very beautiful. Exceptionally good for flower arrangements and formal corsages. M

*LEUCANTHA
Semi-double. Medium large. White form of Tricolor (Siebold). Vigorous, compact growth. Perhaps my favorite white for arrangements. Very cold hardy. M–L

MASTERPIECE
Very large Formal Double to Rose Form Double bloom. Large foliage. Strong, open, upright growth. Good for corsages, but too large for most arrangements. M

*MORNING GLORY
Formal Double. Medium. Compact growth. A favorite of mine because of its perfection of form and medium-size bloom which make it choice for arrangements. Excellent corsage flower also. Very cold hardy. E–M

MRS. CHARLES SIMONS
> Semi-double to loose Peony Form. Large bloom. Spreading growth. Hardy.   M—L

NOBILISSIMA (Fugi-Yama)
> Peony Form. Medium bloom. Upright growth.   E—M

*PURITY
> Formal Double. Large bloom. Beautiful upright growth. Excellent for arrangements, especially appropriate with Christmas Madonnas. Cold hardy.   M—L

QUEEN ELIZABETH (E. H. Rust)
> Semi-double. Medium-size bloom. Upright growth.   L

SHIRO DAIKAGURA
> Peony Form. Medium-size bloom. Compact, upright growth. Exceptionally good arrangement flowers.   E

VICTORY WHITE
> Semi-double to Peony Form. Large bloom. Open, upright growth.   M

WHITE EMPRESS
> Semi-double with fluted petals. Large. Vigorous, compact, upright growth. One of the best plants, but cold often spoils the blooms.   E—M

WHITE HIBISCUS
> Semi-double. Medium large. Upright growth.   E—M

*WHITE QUEEN
> Semi-double with pointed petals. Large. Compact growth. An excellent variety. The long blooming period and beauty of the blooms make it a favorite of mine. Cold hardy. M—L

YOHEI-HOKU (September Morn)
> Semi-double to Peony and Anemone forms. Medium large. White to very pale pink. Compact growth.   E

*YUKI-BOTAN (Pride of Descanso)
> Large. Semi-double to loose Peony Form. Upright growth. Fine for corsages and arrangements when a large flower is desired.   M—L

Plate 10 *Another fine old variety, C. M. Hovey camellias, a formal double, is arranged in a very adaptable black iron compote with a dried root and pine.*

PINK CAMELLIAS

*BERENICE BODDY

Semi-double. Medium. Light pink with deep pink outer petals. Beautiful, dense growth. One of the most cold hardy, and one of the best in size, color and substance for arrangements. Recommended for northern gardens.   M—L

BESSIE MORSE BELLINGRATH (Toki-No-Hagasane)

Semi-double. Large. Blush pink. Upright growth. Cold hardy.   L

BRYAN WRIGHT

Semi-double to loose Peony Form. Medium-size bloom. Compact, upright growth. Unusually fine coloring.   M

CAMEO PINK

Formal Double. Medium small. Compact, upright growth. Beautiful combined with Pink Perfection.   E—M

C. M. WILSON

Peony Form. Large. Spreading growth. Typical of Elegans in form and growth. Shiro Chan, a white sport. Hawaii, pale pink Peony Form.   E—M

*DEBUTANTE

Peony Form. Medium-size bloom. Beautiful, long-lasting light pink. Upright growth. A favorite, fine old variety which should be in every garden, except in the coldest regions. Excellent for arrangements and corsages.   E—M

*DR. TINSLEY

Semi-double. Medium-size bloom. Attractive light pink shading to deeper pink at outer edge. Very compact, upright growth. Superior for all uses. Extremely cold hardy. Recommended for northern gardens.   M

ECLATANTE

Semi-double. Large bloom. Lovely soft pink. Compact growth.   M

*ELEANOR HAGOOD

Formal Double. Medium-size bloom. Pale pink. Nice upright growth. A desirable smaller camellia for arrangements and corsages.   L

GALILEE

Semi-double. Large bloom. Compact growth.   M

HIGH HAT

Peony Form. Large. Light pink. Tall, open growth. A very early bloomer, often the first.   E

HISHI-KARAITO
> Semi-double. Small bloom. Delicate pink. Compact growth. M

KERLEREC
> Semi-double to Anemone Form. Medium bloom. Compact growth. E—M

LALLAROOK
> Formal Double. Medium bloom. Pink with soft white marbling. Slow, compact growth. M—L

*MAGNOLIAEFLORA
> Semi-double. Medium-size bloom. Beautiful blush pink. Slow, compact growth. Highly recommended. Quite cold resistant. M

*MARCHIONESS OF EXETER
> Peony Form. Medium. Open, spreading growth. Combine with Debutante which blooms at the same time. E—M

*MARJORY MAGNIFICENT
> Semi-double to Anemone Form. Medium. Light pink. Compact growth. Very cold hardy and desirable for all uses. Recommended for northern gardens. M—L

*MARTHA BRICE
> Semi-double to Anemone Form. Medium-size bloom. Beautiful lavender pink. Compact spreading growth. Breathtaking in arrangements. M—L

MRS. F. L. GIBSON
> Single. Small to medium bloom. Spreading growth. While the bloom is not large or outstanding it has a very long blooming season and is good in arrangements. E—L

MRS. FREEMAN WEISS
> Semi-double. Large bloom with loose, wavy petals. Compact, upright growth. Popular. Desirable for corsages. M

*NINA AVERY
> Semi-double to loose Peony Form, with high, crinkled center petals. Medium. Beautiful deep pink with white shadings. Very worthwhile. M—L

*PINK CHAMPAGNE
> Full Peony Form. Large bloom. Beautiful salmon pink. Open growth. I have found this variety most outstanding in cold-resistance and quality of bloom. Cold hardy. Recommended for northern gardens. L

*PINK DUCHESS OF SUTHERLAND
> Semi-double of flat form. Large bloom. Compact spreading growth. Good coloring and substance.   M—L

*PINK PERFECTION
> Formal Double. Small bloom. Lovely shell pink. Compact growth. Outstanding for arrangements and corsages when a small, delicate bloom is wanted. Stands cold well.   E—L

*SEMI-DOUBLE BLUSH
> Semi-double. Medium bloom. Blush pink. Spreading growth. Cold hardy.   M—L

SMILING BEAUTY
> Semi-double. Medium. Beautiful delicate pink. Upright growth. Easily hurt by cold.   M

SPRING SONNET
> Peony Form. Large bloom. Pale pink with deeper pink shadings at margin. Upright growth.   M

TALLAHASSEE GIRL
> Semi-double to Peony Form. Medium-size bloom. Soft blush pink. Upright growth.   M

*THELMA DALE
> Semi-double to Rose Form Double. Large. Spreading growth.   M

VIRGIN'S BLUSH
> Semi-double to Peony Form. Medium. Vigorous, upright growth.   M

*WINIFRED WOMACK
> Semi-double. Medium bloom. Open, slightly pendulous growth. Hardy, beautiful and outstanding for arrangements.   M

ROSE COLOR

*ADMIRAL NIMITZ (Kishu-Tsukasa)
> Formal Double. Medium. Upright growth. One of the last to bloom and excellent for colder regions. Cold hardy. M—L

*CASABLANCA (Bleichroeder Pink)
> Rose Form Double. Medium-size bloom. Slow, compact growth. Exceptionally good arrangement flower.   M

III. *Silver scales hold Pink Perfection, Debutante, Lady Clare, Daikagura, Tricolor (Siebold), Are-jishi, George B. Barrett, High Hat and Dawn
(C. vernalis).*

IV.   *A familiar view from my kitchen window. The lead figure of a laughing boy is surrounded by wild fern and elusive woods hyacinths, backed by Rose Dawn camellias and Macrantha azaleas. Baltic Ivy clings to the three-branched tree. This scene offers fascination and delight even when the camellias are no longer in bloom.*

CHRISTINE LEE

Semi-double. Medium. Slow, spreading growth.   M

*DAIKAGURA

Peony Form. Large bloom. Bright rose pink. Slow, compact growth. Very desirable. Also variegated, red and other forms. Long blooming season. Among the first to bloom. E—M

ELEGANS

Anemone Form. Large. Rose pink with center often spotted white. Slow, spreading growth. A good old variety. Cold hardy. Recommended for Northern gardens.   M

ELIZABETH LE BEY

Full Peony Form. Large. Pendulous growth.   E—L

*GENERAL GEORGE PATTON

Rose Form Double. Medium. Upright growth. Cold hardy. M—L

GOVERNOR EARL WARREN

Rose Form Double to Peony Form. Large. Upright growth. M

GUILIO NUCCIO

Semi-double with irregular petals. Outstanding, large bloom. Upright growth.   M

*KUMASAKA

Rose Form Double to Peony Form. Compact growth. One of the best for colder regions. Also variegated and white. Among the last to bloom. Recommended for Northern gardens.   M—L

*LADY CLARE

Semi-double. Very large. Heavy growth. One of the most desirable. Excellent for corsages and arrangements when a large bloom is desired. Should be wired as it loses its head quickly. We have a pair at our back steps which has given us years of pleasure. The large flowers are beautiful against a white house. Cold hardy.   E—M

LADY MARY CROMARTIE

Semi-double to Peony Form. Large bloom. Upright growth.   M—L

LATIFOLIA

Semi-double. Medium bloom. Excellent, fast, bushy growth. Also variegated.   M

LOOK AWAY
> Semi-double bloom. Deep rose at throat with outer border of white. Upright growth.   M

MME. ADELE (Stardust)
> Peony Form. Medium bloom. Upright growth.   M

PINK STAR
> Semi-double with pointed outer petals. Beautiful large bloom. Upright growth.   M

RAINY SUN
> Loose-petaled Semi-double. Medium bloom. Upright growth.   M

REV. JOHN BENNETT
> Semi-double. Large. Spreading growth.   M—L

*REV. JOHN G. DRAYTON
> Semi-double to Peony Form. Medium. Compact, upright growth. Among the last to bloom. Very cold hardy. Recommended for northern gardens.   M—L

R. L. WHEELER
> Semi-double to Anemone Form. Very large, showy bloom. Heavy, upright growth. Also variegated. Excellent large flower for corsages, but too heavy for most arrangements.   M

*ROSE DAWN
> Formal to Rose Form Double. Medium bloom. Slow, spreading growth. Excellent, hardy variety for garden and arrangement.   M—L

*ROSEA SUPERBA
> Rose Form to Formal Double. Large bloom. Upright growth. Especially beautiful for corsages.   M—L

RED

*ADOLPHE AUDUSSON
> Semi-double. Very large. Heavy growth. Also a beautiful variegated. Excellent for any use where a large, heavy, textured bloom is desired.   M

*ARE-JISHI
> Full Peony Form. Large. Dark Red. Upright growth. Usually the first to bloom. A beautiful and showy bloom, but substance often weak. Also variegated.   E

AUNT JETTY
> Semi-double to loose Peony Form. Medium bloom. Full spreading growth.   M

*BEAU HARP
> Peony Form. Large bloom. Upright growth.   M—L

*BLOOD OF CHINA (Victor Emmanuel)
> Semi-double to full Peony Form. Large bloom. Deep Chinese red. Compact growth. Very desirable for all uses. Cold hardy. Recommended for northern gardens.   L

*BRILLIANT
> Rose Form Double. Medium. Compact, upright growth. Also variegated. A good dependable camellia for garden and arrangement. Cold hardy.   M—L

CAMPBELL ASHLEY
> Semi-double. Medium bloom. Upright growth. Also variegated.   L

CHEERFUL
> Formal to Rose Form Double. Medium small. Compact, upright growth. Attractive bloom when not fully open. Cold hardy.   M—L

*C. M. HOVEY
> Formal Double. Large bloom. Upright growth. Long time favorite for all uses.   L

DERBYANA
> Semi-double to Anemone Form. Large bloom. Compact, upright growth. `M—L

*DR. W. G. LEE
> Semi-double. Large bloom. Spreading growth. Cold hardy. M—L

EDWIN H. FOLK
> Semi-double. Large bloom. Bright red. Upright growth. M—L

*FLAME
> Semi-double. Medium to large. Compact, upright growth. Also variegated. Cold hardy.   M—L

FRED SANDER
> Semi-double with curled, fimbriated petals. Large bloom. Compact growth.   M—L

*GLENN 40
> Formal to Rose Form Double. Large bloom. Slow, compact, upright growth. Also variegated. Old favorite. One of the very best all-round camellias. Cold hardy. Recommended for northern gardens.   M—L

Plate 11 *Delectissima camellias, a single form, and gold-sprayed aspidistra dramatize the hand-carved figure of the trumpeter. The dark brown of the burl contrasts with the lighter wood of the figure.*

*H. A. DOWNING

>Semi-double. Large bloom. Bushy growth. Also variegated. Excellent for all uses. Cold hardy. Recommended for northern gardens.   M–L

IMPERATOR

>Peony Form. Medium. Bushy growth.   M

JARVIS RED

>Semi-double. Medium bloom. Salmony red. Spreading growth.   M

JESSIE KATZ

>Semi-double. Large bloom. Unusually creped and wavy petaled. Upright growth.   M

*J. J. PRINGLE SMITH

>Semi-double. Very large. Compact growth. Also variegated. Cold hardy.   M–L

JOSEPH PFINGSTL

>Irregular Semi-double to Peony Form. Upright growth. E–M

KIMBERLEY

>Single, cupped bloom. Medium size. Carmine red with red stamens. Good, compact growth. Cold hardy.   M

*LADY VANSITTART

>Semi-double. Medium. Slow, bushy growth. Also a number of other forms; all good. Cold hardy.   M–L

*LETITIA SCHRADER

>Unusual medallion-shaped Peony to Anemone Form. Large bloom. Compact growth. Also variegated.   M

MARGARET HIGDON

>Semi-double. Medium large. Compact, upright growth.   M

MARION MITCHELL

>Semi-double. Medium. Compact, upright growth. Also variegated.   M

*MATHOTIANA

>Rose Form to Formal Double. Very large bloom. Crimson red often with a purple cast. Upright, compact growth. Early introduced and still considered one of the best. The first camellia I planted and one of my favorites. A number of other forms.   M–L

*MATHOTIANA SUPREME

> Semi-double to Rose Form with stamens and petals interspersed. Very large and showy. Wins top place in many shows. M—L

MRS. CHARLES COBB

> Semi-double to Peony Form. Large bloom. Very dark red. Spreading growth. Also variegated. M

*PAULETTE GODDARD

> Semi-double to loose Peony or Anemone Form. Large bloom. Dark red. Upright growth. Very desirable. Cold hardy. M—L

*PRINCE EUGENE NAPOLEON (Pope Pius IX)

> Formal Double. Medium bloom. Compact, upright growth. An old variety but still one of the best garden camellias. Excellent for corsages and arrangements. This (with Mathotiana and Prof. Charles S. Sargent) was one of my first camellias and I would still choose it for a "first camellia." M

*PROFESSOR CHARLES S. SARGENT.

> Full Peony Form. Medium. Dark red. Compact, upright growth. Also variegated. Does well in colder regions. Handsome in bloom in the garden. M

REG RAGLAND

> Semi-double with mass of yellow stamens. Very large bloom. Compact growth. E—L

SARAH FROST

> Formal Double. Medium. Compact, upright growth. Cold hardy. M—L

ST. ANDRE

> Semi-double to Anemone Form. Large. Bright red. M

TOMORROW

> Semi-double with irregular petals to Peony Form. Very large bloom. Open growth. Very fine. Also other forms. E—M

*VEDRINE

> Anemone to Peony Form. Large bloom. Open, upright growth. E—M

VARIEGATED

AGNES OF THE OAKS

>Semi-double. Large bloom. Deep pink marbled white. Compact growth. E—M

BELLA ROMANA

>Rose Form Double. Medium. Light pink with stripes and splashes of carmine. Bushy growth. M

BETTY SHEFFIELD

>Semi-double to loose Peony Form. Large bloom. White with stripes and splashes of red and pink. Compact growth. A number of other forms. All good. Deservedly popular. M

BROOKLYNIA

>Formal Double. Medium small. Deep pink to pink and white. Bushy growth. Cold hardy. Recommended for northern gardens. L

*CATHERINE CATHCART

>Formal Double. Medium. Pink mottled with white. Slow, open, upright growth. Excellent for arrangement. M—L

*CHIYODA-NISHIKI

>Semi-double. Medium. Pink, softly marbled white and rose. Low, spreading growth. M—L

CLAUDIA PHELPS

>Semi-double of flat form. Large. Soft pink shading to white at outer edges; sometimes splashed white. Compact spreading growth. M—L

COLLETTI

>Peony Form. Medium. Deep red splotched white. Slow growth. E—M

*DAIKAGURA

>Peony Form. Large. Rose pink splotched white. Slow, compact growth. Other forms. E

*DONCKELARII

>Semi-double. Large. Red marbled with varying degrees of white. Slow, bushy growth. An old variety and one of the finest. There are many strains of this camellia. Cold hardy. M—L

DR. JOHN BELL

>Peony form. Large. Dark red heavily variegated white. Upright growth. M—L

ELEANOR OF FAIROAKS

Anemone to Peony Form. Large bloom. Deep red marbled white. Upright, open growth.   E—M

GOVERNOR MOUTON

Semi-double to loose Peony Form. Red splotched white. Cold hardy.   M

HERME

Semi-double. Medium to medium large. Pink with irregular streaks and markings of white and deep pink. Upright growth. There are many forms of this variety including pink, red and white.   M

°IWANE

Semi-double. Medium large. Red marbled white. Slow, bushy growth. One of the best garden camellias. Cold hardy. Recommended for northern gardens.   M—L

°KING LEAR

Semi-double. Large bloom. Red marbled white. Compact growth.   E—M

°LADY KAY

Deep Peony Form, sometimes fimbriated. Large. Red splotched white. Slow, bushy growth. Excellent for garden and corsages. Also deep red.   M—L

°LADY VANSITTART

Semi-double. Medium. White with rose stripes. Slow, bushy growth. Cold hardy.   M—L

LINDSAY NEILL

Semi-double to loose Peony Form. Medium. Dark red marbled white. Compact spreading growth.   E—M

MARGARET NOONAN

Peony Form. Large. Pink striped and splashed rose. Open, upright growth.   M

MARGHERITA COLEONI

Formal Double. Medium small. Deep red splashed white. Upright growth. Also a red form.   L

MME. DE STREKALOFF

Formal Double to Rose Form. Medium. Pink striped white. Upright growth.   M—L

MONJISHU   ·

Semi-double. Medium. Red marbled white. Upright growth.   M

NAGASAKI
>Semi-double. Very large. Rose marbled white. Spreading growth. M

ONIJI
>Semi-double. Very large bloom. Rose red splotched white. Heavy growth. Cold hardy. E—M

SCARLETT O'HARA
>Formal Double. Large bloom. Dark red with spots of white. Upright growth. M

*T. K. VARIEGATED
>Semi-double. Medium. Light pink marked with rose. Compact growth. A fine, old, dependable variety. Cold hardy. Recommended for northern gardens. M—L

*TRICOLOR (SIEBOLD)
>Semi-double, slightly cupped. Medium. White streaked carmine. Very compact growth. One of the finest. Several forms. Cold hardy. Recommended for northern gardens. M

*VILLE DE NANTES
>Semi-double with upright fimbriated petals. Dark red with varying degrees of white marbling. Slow, compact growth. Consistently wins "Best in Show." If I could have only five camellias, this would be one of them. Also a solid red form. M—L

SASANQUAS

CLEOPATRA
>Semi-double. Rose pink. Compact, upright growth.

CRIMSON TIDE
>Semi-double. Ruffled petals. Red.

FLORABUNDA
>Single. White-edged lavender.

HIODOSHI
>Single. Large. Crimson splashed and marbled white.

HUGH EVANS (Hebe)
>Single. Medium-size bloom. Pink.

JEAN MAY
>Double. Large. Shell pink.

KO-GYOKU (Little Gem)
>Rose Form. Double. Medium. Pink, opening pinkish white.

MINE-NO-YUKI (Snow or Snow on Peak)
>Peony Form. Large. White.

NARUMI-GATA (Oleifera)
>Single, cupped. Large. White shaded pink.

ORCHID
>Single. Large. Lavender pink.

PAPAVER
>Single. Large, bell-shaped bloom.

PINK SNOW
>Semi-double. Large. Light pink with lavender traces.

ROSEA
>Single. Medium large. Deep rose pink.

ROSY MIST
>Single. Large. Pink.

SETSUGEKKA
>Semi-double. Large. White.

SPARKLING BURGUNDY
>Peony Form. Large. Ruby rose with lavender sheen.

SPLENDOR
>Semi-double. Very large. Delicate pink with darker pink at edge.

TANYA
>Single. Deep rose-pink.

WHITE GLORY
>Single, with ruffled petals. Large. White.

YAE-ARARE
>Single. Large. White with pink edge.

OTHER SPECIES

ALBA SIMPLEX: *C. saluenensis*
>Single. Small. White.

DAWN: *C. vernalis*
>Semi-double. White, sometimes flushed pink.

DONATION: Hybrid: *C. saluenensis* X *C. japonica*
> Semi-double. Large. Orchid pink. Vigorous, compact, upright growth.

E. G. WATERHOUSE: Hybrid: *C. saluenensis* X *C. japonica*
> Formal Double. Medium. Light pink. Vigorous, upright growth.   M—L

SHISHI-GASHIRA: *C. hiemalis*
> Semi-double to Double. Medium. Red.

SHOWA-NO-SAKAE: *C. hiemalis*
> Semi-double to Rose Form. Medium large. Soft pink, sometimes marbled white.

SHOWA SUPREME: *C. hiemalis*
> Peony Form. Large. Soft pink.

Plate 12 *The camellia is native to open forests, so it does well in this woodland glade in the Bellingrath Garden.*

$\mathcal{P}$LANTING AND CARING FOR CAMELLIAS

The camellia is grown over such widely separated areas with such differing climatic and soil conditions that no single formula is applicable to all regions. Practices common to one area may be impractical in another. It therefore is sensible for growers to keep posted on methods through local as well as national societies. Camellia societies are performing a valuable service in providing correct information for different zones.

Although practices differ from region to region, the basic requirements of good culture are the same the world over. These requirements must be learned well, then the new gardener can adapt them to the needs of his own site.

In its native home, the Far East, the camellia is a hardy woodland plant, growing as a wild undershrub in open forests and in rich, well-drained valleys where it is partially shaded. Its demands are exactly the same as those of many of our wildflowers. The ideal situation is partial shade, uniform moisture, relatively high humidity, good drainage, and a slightly acid, porous soil, well supplied with humus. Camellias will not tolerate deep planting, poor drainage or over-fertilizing.

Once these few basic requirements are met, and healthy plants are set shallowly—with root crown never lower than ground level—in a suitable place in loose, friable soil which will allow quick penetration of water, the growing of camellias presents no difficulty. They will live for years as beautiful, hardy, evergreen shrubs, requiring only a minimum of watchful care.

WHEN TO PLANT

Camellias may be planted at any time of the year when extremely dry, hot weather or hard freeze is not imminent. Even then they may be planted, particularly container-grown plants, if caution is exercised. October through March are generally the preferred months, but the locality must be considered. In the warmer regions, early fall planting is best because it provides sufficient time for the root system to become established before the next summer's heat. In the colder regions, spring planting is preferred.

SOIL

Much care must be given to the proper preparation of the soil and to the correct setting of the plants if success is to be achieved. No amount of aftercare can make up for haste and carelessness at planting time.

The gardener should try to simulate conditions of the camellia's native home by providing the nearest equivalent to forest soil. The camellia tolerates a wide variation in soils, but must have a large percentage of humus. Good sources of humus are acid peat moss, well-decayed leaf mold and well-rotted manure. Peat moss is the best of humus material to mix in the soil because it does not break down quickly and retains moisture exceedingly well. Dampen it thoroughly before mixing with earth.

Any light soil containing fifty percent humus will usually prove satisfactory for camellias. It can be equal parts soil and leaf mold; equal parts soil and leaf mold mixed with peat moss;

equal parts soil and peat moss; or one-half soil, one-fourth peat moss and one-fourth well-rotted manure. In clay or heavy soil, add sand to the soil mixture.

HOW FAR APART TO PLANT

Shrubs which are to grow together as a solid group for hedges or backgrounds should be closely planted. Three to six feet apart is recommended.

Shrubs which must develop perfectly as specimen plants or focal points should be set farther apart. A planting distance of ten or more feet is recommended.

Dwarf types should be planted about three feet apart in a border; taller types are effective four or more feet apart.

LOCATION

Ideally, camellias should have the shifting shade of tall trees or buildings. However, they are not solely shade plants. Many varieties will thrive in full sun and exhibit dense and vigorous growth and a profusion of blooms. Camellias will also grow in full shade, but growth will be open and spindly and the flowers few, although of good size, color and substance.

In cold regions, the location is particularly important. The plants should be protected from sweeping winds, overexposure to the morning sun and fast winter thawing. A western or northern exposure with wind protection is desirable, or a space in the border lightly shaded and protected by tall evergreens.

Every garden and every locality will offer a different problem and require a different solution. Always keep in mind a picture of camellias in their native habitat—wild undershrubs growing on the hillsides or in the well-drained, humus-rich valleys of the Orient.

PLANTING PROCEDURE

Prepare the hole in advance of actual planting by digging it twice as deep and at least twice as wide as the root ball; refill with the prepared soil. Firmly tamp the new soil in the bottom of the hole. Set the camellia plant so that the top of the root ball is two or three inches above ground level. This high planting will insure against the plant being too deep in the ground after it settles. Remember that many plants are killed by deep planting, and it is better to have them too shallow than too deep. Camellias should always be handled by the ball or container, never by the stem. Care must be taken not to break the root ball.

Carefully and firmly pack the soil around the roots. When the plant is set, build a wide, temporary saucer around it and fill with water. As the water is absorbed, fill the saucer again and again, until both plant ball and surrounding earth are thoroughly wet. A newly set plant requires extra water and care during its first year in a new location.

Always keep in mind that conditions do vary; therefore, be observant and try to adapt to each new circumstance.

DRAINAGE

When camellias are planted on a natural slope in porous soil, drainage is no problem. In average garden soil, an adequate drainage system is easily provided by digging the hole for a plant twice as deep and at least twice as wide as the root ball. Under conditions which obstruct drainage—such as a high water table, hopeless brick-like soil or extremely alkaline soil— camellias can be grown successfully in raised beds large enough to allow the roots to spread. Such beds should contain prepared camellia soil, and stand about two feet high. They may be retained and made attractive by the use of old bricks, rocks, or a good border plant such as liriope or ophiopogon.

MAINTENANCE IS EASY

After more than two centuries of culture in the western world, the camellia still has the reputation of a plant difficult to manage and expensive to buy and maintain. Actually a camellia garden can be beautiful, practical and easy to care for; it need not cost more than one planted with other desirable shrubs.

V. *Live oaks festooned with Spanish moss make a natural canopy for a camellia garden, also abloom with azaleas and early spring bulbs. Magnificent iron grillwork frames the picture.* Bellingrath Gardens.

VI.   *Containers collected from many lands hold memories as well as flowers. This ancient Chinese celadon container which I found in Alexandria, Egypt, holds clipped pine, aspidistra, and soft pink Martha Brice camellias.*

It can also be a garden for which considerable amounts are spent on more plants than can be readily cared for.

If the camellia garden has been planned well, varieties carefully chosen and properly planted, maintaining it can be relatively easy.

WATERING

This is one of the most important aspects of growing camellias. How often to water will depend on the climate, the location and condition of the plants, and the soil in which they are planted. Well-shaded and well-mulched plants do not dry out as quickly as those in sunny locations. Wind is also an important factor in drying the soil. Water plantings deeply and well before the soil becomes so dry that it is difficult to get it to drink. Deep watering encourages deep root growth. Frequent light waterings, which fail to wet the ground thoroughly, bring the roots near the surface; this causes damage. Late spring through summer is the most critical period; then the plants need large amounts of water to nourish the lush, new growth and buds. In summer, when there is little rainfall, overhead watering is advisable since plants drink through their leaves as well as roots. In addition to watering, frequent misting of the plant foliage during the very dry weather is beneficial. Do this either early in the morning or late in the day to prevent leaf scald. When buds begin to open, discontinue overhead watering and misting. Instead, soak the roots often and well because the plant needs large amounts of water to properly develop flowers of good size and substance.

Although camellias prefer damp soil, they will not tolerate wet feet. The drainage must therefore be good.

MULCHING

Camellias need a summer mulch for the following reasons: it helps keep the roots cool, helps retain moisture, avoids soil packing, discourages growth of weeds and grass, and keeps soil from washing. Some mulches add acidity and a steady

supply of plant food to the soil as they decay. Others contribute
to the neat appearance of the garden.

Many authorities agree that the mulch should be left on
during the winter. A few say remove it. I don't believe it mat-
ters. If it is left on, and more added from time to time, be
sure the roots do not become too deeply buried over the
years; the mulches decay, and this builds up the soil. This will
kill a plant as surely as deep planting at the outset. I lost a
beautiful, large specimen of Finlandia in this way one year. If
soil is built up too high, rake away extra mulch.

The kind of mulch used depends chiefly on local availability.
The best mulch is pine straw. It gives an attractive appearance;
it is light, clean and easy to place; it does not pack or shed
rain, and it has an acid reaction. Oak leaves, particularly partly
decayed ones, are also excellent. Among other successful
mulches are peanut hulls, sugar cane bargasse, ground corn
cobs, shredded bark, cinders and gravel. Well-rotted manure in
very small amounts is also good.

Peat moss, though an excellent material to mix into the soil
when planting, should not be used as a mulch because it packs
and becomes impervious to water. Cottonseed hulls and sawdust also pack and form a crust that sheds water rather than
absorbs it.

How deep to mulch depends on the material used. A coarse
material can be two or three inches deep; a finer material, only
one or two. Here again, common sense and good judgment
must guide you.

FERTILIZING

There is a difference of opinion concerning the type and
amount of fertilizer to use, when to use it, or even whether
to fertilize at all. Every grower has his pet formula and schedule. The novice, in his enthusiasm, mostly over-fertilizes and
either severely, injures or kills plants. I fertilize very lightly
or not at all.

Camellias in their native environment grow into trees sometimes forty or fifty feet tall by feeding on the leaves and twigs

that fall around them. Plants set in soil containing a good supply of organic matter, which have been mulched with an organic material, need little or no fertilizing unless they are growing in a sandy area where there is constant leaching of food from the soil. Under the latter conditions, they should be fertilized more often. If a commercial fertilizer is used, it should be specifically intended for camellias. The local nurseryman or garden shop will have the prepared mixture best suited to conditions in your area. Follow the directions printed on the package until, with experience, you acquire the know-how to feed according to the need of each plant. Plants should be considered and treated individually, as each has its own characteristics and problems. Never bank fertilizer around trunk of plant. The ground should be moist at time of application and should be watered thoroughly afterwards. In all areas the best time to fertilize is right after the blooming season. In some places a fall feeding is also advised, but in the colder regions this is not a good practice as it encourages a late cycle of growth which might be killed by cold. Several very light feedings, well spaced, are better than one heavy feeding.

Fertilizing can never correct poor cultural practices!

PRUNING

While fertilizing is the most overdone phase of maintaining camellias, pruning is the most underdone and neglected. There are few plants which bear pruning as well as the camellia, and by performing this operation intelligently, you can preserve plants in their proper perspective. Most home gardens are small and only a limited area is available for growing camellias. If plants are kept pruned to five to seven feet, they can be made to fit smaller spaces and can be easily groomed and properly sprayed. The best flowers come from small to medium-size plants.

Pruning can be done at any time, but the best time is during the blooming season and immediately after. Cutting the blooms is one of the best ways of keeping the plants trim. On a small plant, take only an inch or two of stem with each flower; sometimes no stem at all, in which case gently twist off the bloom. On the other hand, entire branches sometimes may be taken with the bloom to help shape the bush. To arrange an entire branch is to exhibit the true loveliness of the camellia. The horticulturist and the flower arranger in me sometimes have terrific battles, and the arranger often wins! The arranger takes flowers of different sizes, including a few partly open. I secure additional foliage from older plants in need of pruning, and by removing irregular or inside branches that would ordinarily be pruned later. These branches are often interestingly shaped in their struggle to reach the light. There is a great variation in form and growth habits of camellias. Some are naturally well-shaped and require little pruning, others are lanky and must be topped and their branches shortened to produce compact growth. An exception is Elegans (Chandler), and its sports, which must never be topped until it has reached the desired height, although the lateral growth can be cut.

Crowded, overgrown and old plants in need of rejuvenation can be cut drastically from top and sides; indeed, they can be cut to the ground and will grow again. The flower-arranging horticulturist will prune by taking foliage and flowers as needed during the blooming season, completing the job at the end of the blooming season. Make cuts back to a growth bud, to a strong branch, or to the trunk in order to prevent stubs.

All the general rules for pruning apply to camellias. Clippers and saws should be sharp. All cuts larger than a pencil should be painted with a tree sealer. Remove all weak, diseased branches, and branches that cross. The centers of plants should be thinned, if needed, to admit light and air, and branches touching or too near the ground should be removed to help control scale.

DISBUDDING

Camellias used in the garden primarily for landscape effect, where a profusion of bloom is desired, should not be disbudded. If exhibition blooms are desired from large-flowered varieties, disbudding can improve the size and quality of the blooms. The proper time to disbud is as soon as flower buds can be distinguished from growth buds. At first the flower and growth buds look very much alike, but as the flower buds develop and become rounded or oval in shape, they can easily be distingished from the slender growth buds.

Disbudding is done by twisting the unwanted bud from the plant, being careful not to injure remaining flower buds and growth buds. The best flowers are produced on the tips of branches, so a general rule is to leave one bud to a terminal. If buds appear down the stem, leave the terminal bud and one other, providing it is spaced far enough down the stem to have room to develop well. Buds left on plant should be at different stages of development to insure a longer blooming season.

Personally I never disbud. In our area, nature does it for us by sending hard freezes.

A camellia grower can give different degrees of physical and mental effort to his chosen plant. There are many intriguing facets of its culture, any of which can offer hours of pleasure. In fact, many backyard gardeners develop into "amateur-experts" on several phases of camellia growing. Camellias can easily turn into an insatiable passion that will lead the gardener over many camellia miles and many camellia roads, along which he will meet some of the nicest people in the world.

$\mathcal{P}$ESTS AND PROBLEMS

Camellias are subject to a number of pests and problems which vary from region to region. Fortunately, most of these can be detected easily and eradicated or controlled. The best way to combat camellia ills is to prevent them: always buy healthy, disease-free plants; plant them carefully, provide adequate care, and give them light, air and good grooming. If, in spite of precautions, problems arise, correct them immediately.

CHEWING PESTS

Several chewing insects feed on camellia plants, but most of them do little damage. Grasshoppers sometimes eat young growth but this is seldom serious. Much damage may be done by a slender, one and one-half inch caterpillar, often referred to as a measuring worm, leaf roller or looper, who feeds on flower buds and young leaves. He is hard to see because of his light green color, and habit of hiding in webs which he makes in a leaf fold or by tying leaves together.

The most destructive chewing insects are snout bettles or weevils which are found only in a few areas. They feed on the leaves at night and hide in the soil during the day. When mature, they lay eggs at the base of the plant, which hatch and develop into grubs that feed on roots, bark and cambium tissues just below the surface of the soil.

To control chewing pests use dimethoate (Cygon) as a spray or as a soil drench. See discussion later in this chapter on systemic insecticides. There are other methods of combating chewing insects. The new growth can be dusted or sprayed with a stomach poison such as lead arsenate, syrolite or chlordane.

SUCKING PESTS

Sucking pests that infest camellias are the scales, aphids and red spider mites. The most persistent and difficult to combat in some areas are the scales. There are several different kinds; all of them are sucking insects which imbed the mouthpiece into the plant tissue and suck the sap from the plant.

Tea scale is the worst, and multiplies and spreads quite rapidly, but is easy to recognize. It infects the undersides of leaves and its feeding causes conspicuous yellowish splotches on the upper surface. An infestation is also characterized by white cottony masses on the underside of leaves.

Camellia scale is another major pest, although not as destructive as tea scale. It looks like a tiny, light to dark brown oyster shell and is also found on the underside of leaves. But it does not discolor foliage. Florida red scale looks like a tiny reddish-brown pinhead and is found on both sides of the leaves. Peony scale mainly attacks the trunk and branches of the plant and is so camouflaged and imbedded into the wood that it is hard to detect. It forms tiny lumps on the bark, and when it dies, falls off leaving light circular spots. There are also other scales which attach to camellias.

SYSTEMIC INSECTICIDES

The most effective control for scales and other camellia pests are systemic insecticides. They are absorbed, translocated to all parts of a plant, including those not directly treated, and render the whole plant toxic to insects. They may be applied any time during the year, but have a maximum effect when applied to plants making new growth. At that time the sap is flowing freely and uptake of the systemic insecticide is rapid. Soil treatments are as effective as sprays, but require a longer time for results.

Dimethoate (Cygon) is the safest and most effective systemic insecticide. It can be used as a spray or as a soil drench. It controls scales, spider mites, thrips, leafhoppers, white flies, aphids, mealybugs and certain leaf miners. Relatively low in toxicity, it may be used safely by anyone who observes routine precautionary meaures.

OTHER SCALE CONTROLS

Scale insects can also be controlled by thoroughly spraying the plants—coating both sides of all leaves—with an oil emulsion such as Volck. Spray in spring as soon as all danger of frost is past, and again in four to six weeks. If heavily infested, the plants should be sprayed again in the fall before the onset of freezing weather. Never apply oil sprays on very hot days, or to dry plants. Malathion may also be used as a spray for scale and at any season of the year.

Other important aids in controlling scale are: continuous pruning of all dead and diseased wood; spraying other plants host to scale, such as euonymus, holly and citrus; and controlling other possible carriers, such as ants. Ants carry and colonize sucking pests, particularly scale and aphids. Eradicate ants in the garden and greenhouse with chlordane dust spread around base of plants or in ant nests.

Aphids and red spider mites are troublesome, but less serious, sucking pests, and can be readily controlled by frequent overhead misting with water or by spraying with nicotine sulphate.

NOTES OF CAUTION

Always read manufacturers' directions on labels and follow

them scrupulously. Experts have worked out formulas that will yield the best results for the plants while providing safety for the user. Store all chemicals in a safe dry place, away from the reach of children and animals.

CAMELLIA FLOWER BLIGHT

Camellia flower blight is a serious problem in some areas. It is caused by a fungus (Sclerotinia camelliae) that produces infective spores in spore-cups that arise from black hard bodies (sclerotia) that were formed on flowers infected during the previous blooming season. These spores are carried by the wind and if they light on open camellia flowers, they germinate, infect the petals and cause blight. It is not passed from one flower to another in the same season, but the spores of the blight fungus are carried by the winds and can infect flowers at a considerable distance, even those in other gardens. Therefore, the only effective way to combat the disease is through a community effort.

Symptoms: Flower blight occurs during the peak of the blooming season. The first noticeable symptoms are small brown spots on the petals of affected flowers. They are most conspicuous on white and pink flowers, but are also evident on darker colors. After a few days, the spots enlarge and eventually most or all of the flower is covered. When the flower is turned over, and the calyx and pistil of the flower are removed, a white to gray ring of cottony fungal growth is usually evident. The texture of the affected flower remains firm when the petal is rubbed between the fingers. After the diseased flower has fallen its base begins to thicken and after about two weeks, hard black bodies, or sclerotia, are formed, taking the general shape of the base of the flower. The presence of these sclerotia is a positive indication of flower blight.

Cold injury may turn blooms brown also, but in cold injury the open blooms turn brown immediately and there are no isolated brown spots. Frost injury can also be easily distinguished from flower blight in that frost injury is restricted to the margins of the petals and flower blight always progresses toward the center of the flower. Flower blight has not been known to develop before mid-January and is most prominent when temperatures range from 50-70° F, and humidity is relatively high.

Control: Once the blight becomes established in an area, it is difficult to combat. The following measures are recommended for keeping the blight in check:

1. *Exclusion.* Balled-and-burlapped camellias should not be moved from blight to blight-free areas. Bare-rooted plants with no open flowers can be safely moved. Also, it is safe to take scions from a blight area provided the scion does not have any open flowers on it.

2. *Sanitation.* All fallen flowers should be picked up at least once a week during the blooming season and burned or buried deeply.

3. *Fungicides.* Investigations have revealed that one can inhibit the germination of the sclerotia, thereby preventing the formation of spores, by applying fungicidal chemicals to the soil and mulch under plants. Of a number of chemicals tested "Terraclor" (pentacloronitrobenzene) gave the best results.

Although it is theoretically possible to get complete control of blight by sanitation or the use of fungicides or a combination of the two, it is not a simple thing to do. A single infected bloom that is not picked up, or one uncooperative neighbor, can undo all the work of many people.

What is needed and hoped for, but as of now does not exist, is a systemic fungicide that can be sprayed on the foliage and which will confer immunity on the bloom for a time. In this way the grower could spray his plants the necessary number of times during the blooming season and be sure that blight would not occur in his garden.

DIEBACK

Dieback, found in a number of districts, is easily recognized.

Twigs or whole branches wilt and die suddenly, but the leaves do not fall at once. Although listed as a fungus disease, some researchers suggest that a nutrient deficiency resulting from over-acidity is a primary cause and fungus only secondary. Dieback is frequently found among plants that have been forced or heavily fertilized.

The only means of control is to remove dead and dying branches, cutting well back into healthy wood. Paint the cut surface, if larger than a pencil, with tree sealer or bordeaux mixture. Practice general cleanliness and good culture.

BUD DROP

Causes for bud drop are many and varied. A sudden change in temperature, particularly a drastic plunge early in the season, will cause buds to drop. Improper drainage, too deep planting, periods of insufficient water, or almost any improper cultural practice, can cause bud drop. Some camellias set too many buds, and the dropping of buds is nature's way of taking care of the situation.

The best cure for bud drop is good culture.

LEAF GALL

Leaf gall is a fungus that usually attacks only sasanquas and appears about the time plants put out new growth. Leaves become thick, fleshy, malformed and greatly enlarged. They turn light green first, and later white. Although leaf gall is very conspicious, and unsightly and alarming to the gardener, it is not serious. The only necessary control is to pick off the enlarged leaves and burn them. Leaf gall is seldom seen by late spring or early summer.

SUNBURN

Too much sun, high temperature, and low humidity will sometimes cause yellow or bronze spots to form on camellia leaves.

These spots may become brown; in some cases, round, dead areas in the leaves may result. Certain varieties are more subject to sunburn than others. Recently transplanted camellias often show sunburn, especially if they are turned in a different direction from their former position.

Keep plants with sunburned leaves well watered and spray the foliage occasionally. If sunburning persists after plant is acclimated, move it to a more shaded location.

LEAF YELLOWING

The life of a camellia leaf is normally about three years. When mature, it turns a golden yellow and falls from the plant. Any other noticeable change in the color of camellia foliage is the sign of an abnormal condition.

General yellowing of camellia foliage almost invariably indicates a lack of water, food, or proper drainage. A yellowing of leaves whose veins remain green indicates lime or alkaline poisoning. This condition usually can be corrected by the addition of iron sulphate, chelated iron, soil sulphur or aluminum sulphate, as recommended by manufacturer. If this condition persists after treatment, replant in new soil.

Some camellia plants may have a yellowish-green or white variegation of the leaves induced by a virus. Thus far, there is no evidence that such variegation harms either plant or bloom.

PEOPLE

The greatest camellia problem is the people who grow it. We are so blinded by the magnificance of the camellia that it is hard for us to realize that it is actually a hardy woodland plant. Fiction and fancy have made the camellia seem fragile and exotic. The delicate-appearing flower often has been mistakenly thought to indicate a delicate plant. Many plants are killed or weakened by too much kindness. Just as pampered, over-indulged and over-protected children do not develop normally, neither do camellias!

The only cure for this camellia problem is common sense.

Their demands are few but exacting. They will not tolerate deep planting, poor drainage or over-fertilizing. Too deep planting kills more plants than any other cause. Over-fertilizing also takes a heavy toll as does poor drainage.

A number of pages have been used in discussing pests and problems of camellias. All that has been said can be repeated in a few sentences. To grow healthy, disease-free camellias practice the following three rules:

1. Good basic culture and common sense.
2. Cleanliness and good grooming.
3. If insects attack, use the latest spray or pest control measure. Today the best general one is Cygon (dimethoate). Tomorrow there may be something better.

While the world of gardening and flowers remains basically the same generation after generation, mechanical gadgets, insecticides, sprays, fertilizers, etc. change our ways of gardening. Regardless of the changes in camellia-growing methods, the need for good basic cultural practices, cleanliness and common sense will never change.

Plate 13   *A lath house protects tubbed Camellia reticulatas from the sun. Here the plants are exhibited amongst decorative rocks and river gravel at the home of Mr. F. S. Tuckfield, Berwick, Victoria, Australia.* Photo courtesy Mr. Tom Savige.

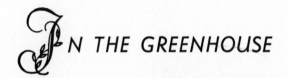N THE GREENHOUSE

To those with a greenhouse, stepping into a warm "garden" in the middle of winter is as exciting as a trip on a magic carpet, and far easier to achieve. Although Paul and I do not own a greenhouse, we asked our friends, Mrs. William P. Kemp and Mrs. Frank Dowd, both camellia growers and greenhouse enthusiasts, to enrich our *Treasury* with this chapter on cultural practice.

One need not grow prize-winning blooms to enjoy a greenhouse. Great satisfaction and pleasure can be derived from having a few plants whose flowers are safe from winter's freezes. A greenhouse as an auxiliary to a garden is just as important as one used to grow specimen blooms for competition.

CONTAINER CULTURE

Most greenhouse plants are grown in containers. Many more plants can be included in a limited space, and can be quickly replaced if newer varieties become desirable. The size of the plant is readily controlled by pruning both the roots and branches.

Another advantage is that all plants can be grown in soil requiring uniform care. This soil may be easily renewed or eventually replaced. For growing prize blooms, the soil should be renewed after three or four years for top performance.

In summer, the containers can be carried outdoors and set beneath the trees or in a lath house (Plate 13). Here they should be well mulched to conserve moisture. Many people prefer to remove the mulch when the plants are moved indoors, making it easier to check the dampness of the soil and avoid the possibility of harboring insects.

Of the many kinds of containers, the most satisfactory seem to be made from wood or metal. Wooden containers look best, but are expensive and deteriorate quickly. Metal containers may be obtained in various sizes and are easy to handle. They can be made more durable and more pleasing to the eye by being painted a uniform color with rust-resistant paint.

DRAINAGE

Drainage is perhaps the most essential part of the culture. To provide proper drainage, punch holes about five or six inches apart around the outer edge of the can near the bottom. Cans larger than three gallons should also have three or four fairly large holes in the bottom. Place coarse material of small stones or crushed rock in the bottom of the cans to prevent these drainage holes from becoming blocked. Add small pieces of charcoal for efficiency and to help sweeten the soil.

One of the secrets of healthy plants is to place them in a container which is not too large when understock is small. Excess soil becomes sour and may cause root rot. It is better to have plants in a can too small rather than too large.

BAREROOTING AND PLANTING

When planting in containers, barerooting is essential. When plants reach a dormant stage in mid-August or September, bare-

VII. *Four graduated crystal cake stands are stacked in the form of a compote for a large dining-room table. The camellias are: Lady Clare, Debutante, Are-jishi, Pink Perfection, Daikagura, George B. Barrett and Dawn* (C. vernalis).

VIII.   *An ancient oriental bronze container holds aspidistra leaves and
Blood of China blooms—still one of the best varieties for the garden. The
base is an old Japanese burl.*

root them by gently running a small stream of water over the ball or soaking in a tub. In this way, heavy clay or sticky muck from field-grown plants can be safely removed. This prevents plants from becoming root-bound in the heavy soil. Another advantage is that latent sclerotia and consequent spread of petal blight are avoided. Care must be taken not to injure the fine hair roots. Roottone may be added for greater safety. This process also gives an excellent opportunity to examine the roots. Cut off the weak and broken ones and cut back the top in balance with the root system.

Place the plant in the container so that the roots come within two inches of the edge of the can. The old precept still holds: Be careful not to plant too deep! For small plants an easy rule is that the depth of planting should approximate the diameter of the can. Add an inch of soil above the drainage material at the bottom before placing the plant in the container. Then add soil, a little at a time, jarring the can frequently to be sure the soil is thoroughly worked through the root system. When roots are barely covered, the plant should be well watered, then left to settle.

The soil on the top should be level; if it is mounded, the water may run off before reaching the roots. Allow three to four inches at the top of the can for space to add fertilizer, water, mulch, etc. Take care to keep the roots from drying out during the process, which is best done in a cool, shady spot. After planting, the leaves should be sprayed with water once a day for thirty days or more, preferably late in the afternoon to conserve the moisture and prevent dehydration of foliage.

Expert growers differ in the choice of soil mixtures, as good cooks differ in their recipes, but the results are equally good. Here are two concoctions; take your pick. Both have often won "best in show" as well as produced many choice blooms.

One excellent grower uses one-third peat moss, one-third well-rotted cow manure (over two years old), and one-third sand. Another uses two parts sterile soil free of clay, one part imported peat moss (it decomposes slowly and makes fine organic material) and one part ground pine bark. Then he adds enough coarse, sharp builder's sand to provide immediate drainage. Usually, one-half part sand will be sufficient.

It is essential to have a porous soil with large amounts of humus because of the small space in which plants are grown. This assures good drainage and the right medium for carrying fertilizer to the roots. The soil should have the capacity to retain moisture as well, and should have a pH of 5 to 6.5, although a slightly higher variation is tolerable.

FERTILIZING

Methods of fertilizing also vary widely. Each grower has a pet formula and few agree on the best one. Like the Irishman's whiskey, "they are all good, but some are better than others."

Many breath-taking beauties have been grown with the following program.

1. Two general feedings of well-balanced azalea and camellia fertilizer containing the important trace elements. Apply after blooming, and then again six to eight weeks later.

2. Quantity: one heaping tablespoon to a three-gallon container; proportionate amounts for larger tubs. After application, lightly scratch the soil to prevent glazing and to afford even penetration.

3. In the spring, foliar feed with prepared liquid fertilizer, combined with good insecticide, every three weeks until new growth is hardened. Consult directions and use less than the amount suggested. Remember, strong new growth determines to a great degree the quality of future blooms.

4. Return plants to greenhouse November 1; climate determines one's individual program. After first hard freeze, begin to fertilize every three to four weeks with liquid preparation. Never apply fertilizer until plant is thoroughly saturated with water. To thirty gallons of water, add two-thirds pint of 15-5-5 liquid plant food which contains fish meal derivatives; two quarts of dried blood, and ten to twelve tablespoons of iron sulphate or equivalent. Apply sparingly, one pint of mixture to a three-gallon container, increase proportionately for larger tubs. Continue this program until greenhouse is nearing height of blooming period, then water copiously to assist the plant which is straining towards optimum

bloom. Camellia flowers are over 90% water in composition. At blooming time they consume more than normal amounts of water, and transpire even more rapidly.

5. In September, give a small quantity of 0-14-14 dry fertilizer and a small quantity of cottonseed meal: one tablespoon to a three-gallon container. However, we are not convinced that a high content of phosphorous and potash in combination alone, that is, without nitrogen, is of great benefit.

Fertilizer is best applied to moist soil, followed by thorough watering. Container-grown plants should never be allowed to become dry, but kept preferably on the moist, not wet, side.

FOLIAR FEEDING

The spray gun is valuable for use in foliar feeding. Several excellent soluble fertilizers on the market, such as Plant Marvel, Rapid-Gro, and Vigoro, can be sprayed over the foliage to keep it green and healthy. This liquid fertilizer is absorbed into the plant, and is easy and absolutely safe to apply. Spray in the early morning or late afternoon, never during the heat of the day. Foliar feeding is a supplement to your regular feeding program. It should be terminated in June so that plants may harden properly in time to prevent winter damage.

GIBBERELLIC ACID

Mrs. Frank Dowd is very enthusiastic over her experiments with Gibberellic Acid. She reports sensationally large blooms of greatly improved form and beautiful deep color produced weeks before normal blooming time. While her experiments so far have been with greenhouse flowers, she feels that use of Gibberellic Acid will be a boon to the out-of-doors grower who will be able to bloom many varieties in the fall that normally bloom in mid-winter. This will result in bigger and better camellia shows, especially in the fall.

Formula: Many growers mix their own formula, but Mrs. Dowd has her pharmacist mix hers, which is easier and not expensive. There are several variations of the formula but the one that sounds simplest to me is as follows: 20 milligrams of 85% Gibberellic Acid to 1½ cubic centimeters of distilled water. Since Gibberellic Acid is not soluble in water but is soluble in weak alkaline solution, add household ammonia a drop at a time, shaking between drops, until the solution clears and the Gibberellic Acid no longer settles to the bottom of the vial. Although the Gibberellic Acid needs no special storing when in powder form, it should be refrigerated after it is in solution.

Procedure: Gently pull out growth bud adjoining a well-developed flower bud, leaving a little cup. Using a medicine dropper, fill the resulting cup with Gibberellic solution. There seems to be no advantage in treating a bud more than once. Mrs. Dowd started some buds early in September and proceeded to fertilize other buds every two weeks in order to have a succession of bloom.

Warning: While miraculous results are experienced in many cases, some varieties do not respond to this treatment. Generally, rose form varieties respond wonderfully, but anemone forms do not.

Treat only a few buds on each bush. Do not treat the chosen few at one time, but at intervals of two or three weeks to insure a long blooming season. Some aspects of the treatments are untried, so go slowly in your experiments.

Mrs. Dowd cuts "Gibbed" blooms two leaves down from treated bud as a precaution against possible plant injury from use of Gibberellic Acid.

While the method of fertilizing buds to produce huge flowers is new with us, the Chinese and Japanese have practiced it for a very long time. This is an exciting aspect of camellia growing, but only time will tell whether treatment with Gibberellic Acid is a passing fad or the dawn of a new era in camellia culture. One thing is certain. The use of "Gib" will not eliminate the need for proper camellia culture.

HUMIDITY

A high relative humidity may be furnished through the use of a mist spray on the foliage in the late afternoon. After the

Plate 14 *"Wintershed" is a well designed and efficiently arranged greenhouse owned by Mr. and Mrs. Jack H. Brown, Greensboro, N. C. Here, camellia plants are brought to full bloom, then moved into a charming enclosed patio for the pleasure of the owners and their many friends who are camellia fanciers.* Martin's Studio photo.

bloom opens, condensation of moisture on the petals injures and discolors the bloom, so humidity must be supplied elsewhere. The best results are achieved by covering the floor with a three inch layer of sand, an intermediate layer of sawdust, and a top layer of pea gravel or small white stones. This should be kept wet at all times. Stepping stones may be used between plants.

Fine automatic humidifiers now on the market may be better. We, however, have had no experience with them.

SHADING AND WATERING

The usual high, filtered sunlight is good for indoor growing, too; but if there is too much sunlight, Saran shade cloth, available in a wide range of densities, may be used when necessary and then easily stored. Plants may be removed from the greenhouse in April and placed in partial shade. During the summer, they may be cooler and have better air circulation out-of-doors.

Plants require frequent watering, at least once a week during the summer, when buds are setting. They should be placed indoors again before the first hard freeze in the fall. In the greenhouse, water only once every two weeks, and if possible, mist spray briefly each day to raise the humidity.

During the blooming season more water is required since the flowers themselves contain a large percentage of water. Too much water, however, may lead to bull-nosing.

PRUNING AND DISBUDDING

Pruning is another of the secrets of prize winners. The best time to prune is right after the blooming season and before new growth starts; in a greenhouse, however, any time is a good time if necessary. Plants cut back in early spring put forth vigorous, healthy, new growth on which the best buds are set. Prune plants to conform to your needs. If upright growth is encouraged, much space may be saved.

Since indoor culture is highly specialized and many blooms are grown as specimens, the best results are obtained when plants are heavily disbudded. A general rule is to leave only one bud to a terminal. Begin as soon as the flower buds appear; the sooner the better.

Plants can be kept small and adapted to containers by systematic root pruning, removing a few roots from plants each year.

TEMPERATURE

Greenhouses should be kept on the cool side, always above freezing, but never warmer than 40° F. for low morning temperatures. Daytime temperatures should be kept at 50° if possible. High temperatures cause bud drop and inferior bloom. There must be some means of ventilation through the top of the house, since warm air rises. Use an automatic ventilating system, or manipulate by hand.

SPRAYING

Since culture is so concentrated, spraying against disease is very important. Scale is one of the problems, as are insects. The average grower with a hundred plants or less can easily control plant pests with an ordinary garden hose attached to a spray gun. Several excellent sprayers are available. Simply remove the garden hose nozzle, and replace it with the sprayer. Your favorite garden supply dealer has the chemicals and abundant information on how and when to use them. Malathion is excellent for controlling aphids, red spider mites and other pests. Follow the mixing directions carefully.

A product recently made available, Cygon (dimethoate) readily controls most scales and pests. Possibly the easiest method of application is to mix Cygon in the ratio of one teaspoon to one gallon of water, and soak the root system of the plant. An ordinary watering can instead of the sprayer is satisfactory. The pest-killing agent in Cygon is picked up through the root system of the plant, and distributed to all parts including the leaves. Follow directions for intervals of application.

Work in a glass house is interesting and can be a real labor of love. The amount of TLC (tender, loving care) given the plants seems to hold the secret of success. The rewards are varied; great satisfaction and pleasure come from having beautiful blooms to wear, to exhibit, or to share. It is always a thrill to have lovely white camellias for a bride's bouquet, or a rare bloom to carry to an ill or bereaved friend. After all, camellias are more eloquent than human beings!

VARIETIES FOR THE GREENHOUSE

All varieties of camellias grow larger under glass. This is especially true of the white camellias which are easily spoiled by wind and rain.

Mrs. Frank Dowd lists the following personal choices for greenhouse culture.

VILLE DE NANTES
> She lists this good standard variety first. It grows well outdoors, but to perfection in the greenhouse. Men just can't resist it. Dark red splotched white. Large. Semi-double. M–L

TOMORROW and the other members of its family:
TOMORROW SUPREME, TOMORROW'S DAWN, and the variegated form
> Tomorrow is red, Tomorrow Supreme is predominantly white, Tomorrow's Dawn is a deep, soft pink shading to white at edges. All are magnificent. Large. Semi-double. E–M

BETTY SHEFFIELD SUPREME
> White with deep pink to red borders on petals. Semi-double to Peony Form. There are a large number of sports of Betty Sheffield, all different and all good, but this is *really* supreme. The most unusual camellia today.   M

GUILIO NUCCIO

A magnificent coral rose, has great style. A California seed-
ling and winner of the John Illges Medal. Semi-double.
Large. It is not unusual for blooms to measure 6 or 7 inches.
Also variegated.   M

MRS. D. W. DAVIS

Another John Illges Medal winner. The very large, blush
pink blooms have an angelic quality that takes your breath
away. Semi-double.   M

REG RAGLAND

An impressive, large, Semi-double red bloom. The variegated is more outstanding than the red and is a John Illges
Medal winner. A long blooming season.   E–L

MATHOTIANA SUPREME

Very large, crimson bloom with great depth. Also variegated. There are a number of Mathotiana sports, but this
is the best.   M–L

CORAL PINK LOTUS

Very large, Semi-double. Coral pink with darker pink
veins. Beautiful, but quite fragile and does not hold up
well.   M

CORONATION

The most spectacular white, whose magnificent blooms
often measure 6 and 7 inches. Semi-double.   M

DRAMA GIRL

Very large, Semi-double. Deep rose pink. Also variegated.
M

Mrs. Dowd also recommends CARTER'S SUNBURST (Pink.
E-L), FROSTY MORN (White. M-L), WINTER MORN
(White. M), DIXIE KNIGHT SUPREME (Deep red, heavily

variegated. M-L), JULIA FRANCE (Pink with an orchid cast. M), ROSEA SUPERBA (Crimson, also variegated. M-L); ALBA PLENA (White, E-M), MRS. HOOPER CONNELL (Peony Form of Alba Plena), DIDDY MEALING (White with a streak of pink. M) and KATHERINE MARYOTT (Pink. L); R. L. WHEELER (Rose pink. M-L) and other members of this family, and WHITE NUN (White. M).

The *reticulata* species, which cannot be grown outdoors, are magnificent in the greenhouse. CRIMSON ROBE, NOBLE PEARL and BUDDHA are the best known varieties. The Reticulatas are in a class by themselves. There are also a number of fine hybirds. The popular DONATION is a good garden plant. CHARLEAN is a new sensation.

7

*B*ONSAI AND OTHER
CONTAINER-GROWN CAMELLIAS

BONSAI

In the true Japanese sense, bonsai is a process of dwarfing plants by careful training over many years, so that they have in miniature the character of a gnarled, old specimen. In the western adaptation of bonsai, a plant is first potted and then its branches pruned into fanciful shapes to give it a look of picturesque naturalness.

Most japonicas are too large for this work. The naturally dwarf, low-growing sasanquas, such as Mine-No-Yuki and Tanya, are excellent, as are hiemalis Shishi-Geshira and Showa-No-Sakae. When buying a plant for bonsai, search for one as stunted and misshapen as possible.

In bonsai, as in Japanese flower arranging, the choice of container is important. Bonsai plants are traditionally grown in shallow trays or bowls of many shapes and sizes.

The soil mixture for bonsai camellias is not the same as that for other container-grown plants, or for those grown in the ground. Good garden loam combined with ten percent sand and

Plate 15 *A healthy and attractive small potted specimen plant of Elegans (Chandler) in full bloom.* Paul E .Genereux photo.

ten percent fine leaf mold to which charcoal is added is a good general mixture.

When setting the plant, work in a cool, shaded location, making sure to keep the roots from drying out. Wash all dirt carefully from the roots. Usually it is necessary to prune them to fit the container. Prune the main branches of the plant in such a way as to emphasize its structure. Then place a piece of screen wire over the drainage hole and spread a thin layer of soil over the bottom of the container. Place the plant in the container at its most picturesque angle. Add the soil slowly, pressing it firmly about the roots; be sure to fill the pot uniformly. Water the plant carefully and well.

If a branch or stem does not conform to the desired pattern, tie or wire it to trunk or to another branch or stem. After several months, the wire can be removed and the stem will be permanently bent.

Maintaining a bonsai is not easy. At no time should it be exposed to hot sun, drying winds or severe cold. Nor should it be kept in the greenhouse where growth would be unnaturally forced. Bonsai camellias must be kept protected—under trees, against walls, under lath—and convenient to water. The watering of bonsai plants can be a real chore; one day without water can mean the death of a plant and the destruction of many years of work. For special occasions, a bonsai plant may be brought into the house but must not be allowed to remain long, because of lack of proper amounts of light and humidity.

Do not fertilize. When a plants shows need of food, remove it from the pot, wash away most of the soil and repot in new soil.

For the person with the time and patience to train and care for camellias in this manner, bonsai can be a fascinating hobby. Camellias so dwarfed can be exquisite works of art.

CONTAINER-GROWN CAMELLIAS

Camellias in containers are popular for outdoor as well as greenhouse use. Select varieties as a definite part of the landscape scene, not as a collection of kinds and colors. Camellias in containers can be arranged and rearranged as they bloom, creating diverse and charming effects. They may be placed along walls and terraces, around patios, and at steps and entrances to accentuate the garden décor.

In a small garden it is possible to grow in containers a greater number of camellias than could be grown only in the ground.

Potted camellias can be moved from greenhouse to patio during the blooming season, from outdoors to indoors during a freeze. In summer they can be placed in an area shielded from the sun and wind, where they can be easily watered and cared for. Containers make plants portable, so that gardeners who must move can take their flowers with them.

Soil and other requirements of container-grown camellias are specified in the chapter "In the Greenhouse."

CAMELLIAS AS HOUSE PLANTS

Camellias are not suitable for house plants in the average home. If there is a place available where room temperature can be kept between 35° F. and 50° F., a high humidity maintained, and the proper amount of light supplied, potted camellias may be grown successfully.

HANGING BASKETS

A container specialty is the hanging basket. The best choice of container is a redwood tub, which will help retain moisture. The low-growing, pendulous varieties, such as Sweet and Low, Chiyoda-Nishiki, and the sasanquas Mino-no-yuki and Tanya, are easy to train for such use.

Mr. Harvey F. Short of La Mesa, California, well-known throughout the camellia world for fine seedlings and introductions, has experimented with special uses of plants; I am indebted to him for several of the ideas in this chapter. Mr. Short is developing some dwarf-type japonicas with pendulous habit and interesting flowers, to be used in hanging baskets.

Plate 16 *Camellias in many kinds of containers and varied stages of growth shown at the home of Mrs. C. G. Fairley, Glen Iris, Victoria, Australia. Note the beginning of a bonsai at the right.* Photo courtesy Mr. Tom Savige.

One is being cultivated for its gorgeous foliage effect, a clear and rich mahogany red. The foliage coloring lasts about two months before turning dark green. It also has a black-red formal flower with pointed petals. This and other exciting new developments will furnish interesting accents to the garden scene.

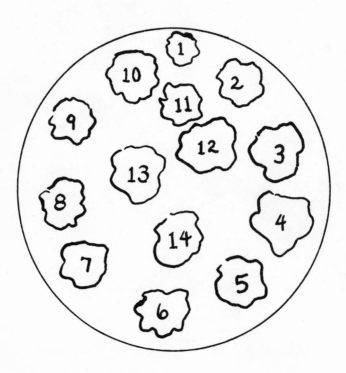

IX. 1. Pink Perfection   8. Eleanor Hagood
     2. Donckelarii   9. Ville de Nantes
     3. September Morn   10. Oniji
     4. Lady Clare   11. Berenice Boddy
     5. Seedling (my own, unnamed)   12. Nagasaki
     6. Debutante   13. George B. Barrett
     7. High Hat   14. Marchioness of Exeter

X. *Lady Clare, High Hat, and variegated Daikagura camellias with white snapdragons, secured in a large cup holder. I waxed the interior of the container to protect the alabaster, which is easily damaged by water.*

8

ROPAGATION

Everyone who loves and grows camellias will at some time want to propagate them himself. I find this a stimulating and fascinating aspect of camellia culture. They are propagated from seeds, by rooting cuttings, grafting and air-layering. The fundamentals of each method are easily learned.

SEEDS

Although camellias do not come true from seeds and it is not possible to perpetuate a specific variety by this means, there is always the exciting possibility that a wonderful new variety will be produced. The majority of seedlings have small single or relatively small semi-double blooms of no particular value, but these seedlings are desirable also because they make excellent understock on which to graft wanted varieties.

The time for harvesting camellia seeds varies from region to region. Usually, they ripen in late summer or early fall, when the seed pods begin to open. To prevent a loss of seeds, gather them as soon as a few of the pods begin to split. The pods can either be forced open or spread on a collecting tray and left to open on their own; within a week or two all the pods will split and the seeds can be collected.

Seeds should not be allowed to dry out. Dry seeds are slow and sometimes impossible to germinate. If gathered from half-open pods and planted quickly, they will germinate in a very short time. If it is not convenient to plant seeds when they are gathered, store them in a tight jar in the refrigerator until they can be planted.

The simplest method of germinating camellia seeds is to place them in damp peat moss or some other medium in a covered, wide-mouth glass jar. The seeds germinate over a period of two to eight weeks. The first indication of activity is the appearance of a small white radicle which is the primitive taproot. When the taproots are one to two inches long, remove seeds from the jar and pinch off about half the taproot. Then plant the tiny seedling root down, in pots or, if there are many, in a flat. Plant so that just the tops show, in equal parts sand and vermiculite, or equal parts sand and damp peat moss.

The taproot soon will callus and many little feed roots will develop. As this process takes place, a small young stem appears at the top of the radicle. The stems quickly develop leaves, and within three or four months the young plants are several inches tall. Leave them in the sand mixture six months or longer and then plant in individual pots or in growing beds. The principal care seedlings require during the first few months is watering. There is sufficient food in the seed itself to supply the plant for several months.

Under normal conditions, the seedling blooms in four to seven years. However, some seedling propagators have brought seedlings into bloom in less than eighteen months by elaborate scientific techniques, not recommended for most of us.

CONTROLLED POLLINATION

Many of our choicest varieties have been produced by natural pollination, but the chances of producing a superior bloom in this way are remote. Most seedlings have blooms inferior to

Plate 17　*This charming seedling camellia espaliered against a wall is courtesy of Mr. Myron Kimnach, Superintendent of the Huntington Botanical Gardens, San Marino, California.*

their parents in color, size and form. However, the possibility
of obtaining a fine new variety from seeds can be stepped up
considerably by controlled pollination. Many good new camellias come from backyard gardeners who are practicing controlled pollination. They simply transfer pollen from the stamens of one selected variety to the pistils of another.

To cross-pollinate camellias, choose as female parent a flower
which is well developed but not yet open. Open the flower carefully by hand, and with small scissors remove all the pre-ripe
pollen-bearing anthers. This is to prevent self-pollination. Care
must be taken not to injure the pistil at the center of the bloom.
Cover the emasculated flower with a waxed paper bag to protect it from undesirable fertile pollen which might be carried
by insects or wind. Gather the bag close around the stem and
fasten it with a wire or clip. Examine the stigma at the top of
the pistil two days later. If it is covered with a sticky substance,
which catches and retains pollen, it is receptive and ready for
the pollen from the selected male parent. Take the pollen from
the male parent flower with a soft brush and apply it freely to
the pistil of the other parent. Then recover the latter with the
waxed paper bag and label with date, female parent and male
parent.

If the cross is successful, the ovary will begin to swell very
soon after pollination. Leave the bag on until this swelling is
noticeable.

In selecting parents, it may be desirable to cross varieties of
different blooming seasons. This can readily be done by gather-
ing pollen and storing it in small medicine capsules. Label and
place these capsules inside a sealed bottle and keep in a cool,
dry place under constant temperature.

I have been content to cross only different varieties of a
single species, C. *japonica*, but for the amateur hybridizer em-
barking on a wider program, C. *saluenensis* is considered the
best species to use as a seed parent. C. *saluenensis* produces
seeds freely and tolerates a wide number of species as pollen
parents. Its bushy and compact growth habit seems to be trans-
mitted to any cross in which it is used as seed parent. It has

shown cold hardiness when crossed with *C. japonica*, and its flowers invariably have a striking, translucent beauty. Seedlings of *C. saluenensis* will produce flowers in the second or third year; normally, seedlings require from four to seven years to produce the first bloom.

Mr. J. C. Williams was the first to cross this species with *C. japonica*, and seedlings from *C. saluenensis X. C. japonica* subsequently carry the collective name Williamsii. The best known of the Williamsii hybids are J. C. Williams and Donation. These varieties have a great deal of vigor, are quite bushy and compact in habit, produce exquisite flowers in great profusion, and are outstanding in cold hardiness. Their cold hardiness is greater than that of either parent.

Mr. E. G. Waterhouse of Australia has made some excellent *C. saluenensis X C. japonica* crosses. The best of these, a long lasting, formal double pink, bears his name. Two others are Margaret Waterhouse and Lady Gowrie.

CUTTINGS

Propagation by cuttings is popular because of its simplicity, economy and predictability. Cuttings always come true to the parent plant.

All that you need to start is a cutting box covered with polyethylene or an airtight cold frame, and a rooting medium. One-half sharp sand and one-half vermiculite or peat moss, or just pure sand, are used.

Cutting box: A common wooden box eight to twelve inches deep, or a regular seed flat if it is rigged with eight to twelve-inch sticks at each corner to support a polyethylene cover, will simulate a small greenhouse. The bottom of the box or flat should have sufficient holes or cracks to allow good drainage of water. To prevent loss of the propagation medium, first cover the holes with screen wire, or fill them with sphagnum moss. The plastic cover should be large enough to tuck under the edges of the flat after the cuttings are inserted. This helps retain high humidity during the rooting period. The flat of cut-

tings should be placed to catch filtered sunlight, such as under
trees or shrubs.

Cold frames: If a cold frame is used, be sure it is located
on well-drained soil, facing south, and placed under light
shade trees or provided with a similar amount of shade. Fill bottom of frame with two inches of gravel for drainage, and over
this place two inches of sand to hold moisture and build up
humidity. To insure good drainage and circulation of air around
them, set flats on strips of wood or on bricks which have been
partially sunk in the sand and gravel. After the flats are placed
in the cold frame and filled with cuttings, thoroughly soak both
flats and sand. To provide the humid atmosphere essential
during the rooting period, the sand in the bottom of frame
must be watered frequently. After the first watering, the flats
should be kept moist, but not saturated. In a tight cold frame
only frequent watering of the sand floor will be necessary. The
flats occasionally may need a fine mist of water sprayed over
them.

Take cuttings either early in the morning or after a rain.
Use a sharp knife or pruning shears. Set immediately, or
keep cool and moist by wrapping in a damp cloth or paper.
Select for rooting the terminal ends of well-seasoned new
growth from healthy, vigorous plants. Whether the wood is
sufficiently well-seasoned can be determined by examining its
color and substance; when right for cuttings the branches are
brownish in color and will snap back quickly if bent between
thumb and finger. The length of cuttings will depend on the
variety, the amount of current growth and the scarcity of the
wood. It is possible to root a cutting with only one leaf and
one growth bud, but ideally it should be four or five buds in
length. The buds are borne at the base of each leaf; therefore,
a shoot with four or five buds would have four or five leaves.
Remove all the leaves on the lower part of each cutting,
leaving two or three at the tip. These may be cut in half to
save space and to reduce transpiration. Before putting it to
root, make a long, clean cut at the base of the cutting just
below the last growth bud. Dip the cut first in water, then in

root-inducing hormone powder (follow directions on the package). Insert the cutting into the rooting medium, which has been thoroughly wet and packed into the frame. A furrow to receive the cuttings can be cut with a knife. Insert prepared cuttings at a forty-five degree angle with their leaves above the medium, far enough apart so they do not touch each other. Tamp well, label each row as to variety and date, water thoroughly and cover tightly; place in a rooting box or unheated cold frame. They will root in two to eight months depending on variety; some root quickly and easily, others are slow and difficult. The only attention they require during the period of rooting is misting with water as often as necessary to insure high humidity within the enclosure. The soil around the cutting should be moist but never soggy. Thoroughly water the cuttings at time of setting; do not water again until the surface of the medium shows signs of slight drying, then water thoroughly again.

Cutting boxes may also be set in the greenhouse to root. No matter what type cover is used, avoid high temperatures. Careful shading of cold frame or greenhouse must be practiced.

Commercial growers and others rooting large numbers of cuttings often use more complicated methods. Some also prefer semi-hard cuttings which they can root in six to eight weeks. Amateurs find hardened-wood cuttings easy to handle and much more satisfactory. A rooting box, cold frame, or a simple glass jar turned over a large pot, will maintain the high humidity and close atmosphere the cuttings require and provide the home gardener with remarkable success.

Transplanting: The little plants can be transplanted into pots or into growing beds anytime after they have developed good root systems, however, I often leave them in flats for months. When the cuttings have rooted they should be hardened off by gradually letting in more and more air until they no longer require a protective covering.

Cuttings bloom usually in three to five years.

GRAFTING

I find grafting the fastest and most exciting way of propagating camellias. It is an invigorating experience to change a seedling or a common unwanted variety into a rare and improved cultivated variety—a cultivar.

There are many methods of grafting, but the cleft graft has proved to be the most dependable and successful method for camellias. It requires simple tools, techniques and after-care. It is best done in January, February and March in America. In the southern hemisphere, the reverse seasons would change this time to June, July and August. Grafting is a plain and simple procedure, and any amateur with patience can successfully graft from the first attempt.

The necessary tools are a sharp knife, a small sharp saw, a wide-bladed kitchen knife or a grafting chisel, a screwdriver, a small hammer. Also, a large (gallon size) wide-mouthed jar, a paper bag or burlap sack that will fit over the jar, some builder's sand, and a small quantity of Captan or Fermate.

Scions: The scion, or cutting, is chosen like any other cutting from the healthy, hardened tip growth of the desired variety, and cut about three inches long with two or three growth buds. If the variety is very new or scarce, inside wood with only one leaf and growth bud to each scion may be used. However, tip cuttings with several growth buds insure a better, bushier specimen. As with cuttings, scions must be kept cool and moist until used. If necessary, they can be kept for days or weeks by placing in a plastic bag with a few drops of water and tightly sealing them. It is possible to transport scions or send them by mail by thus sealing and shipping in a cardboard box.

Understock: Select a strong, well-rooted, healthy plant for understock. This is usually a seedling, a common sasanqua or an ordinary japonica. Any healthy plant growing in the ground or in a container, that has not been recently transplanted or fertilized, is suitable. The understock will provide the mechanism for the nourishment of the new plant. The best results are usually obtained from well-grown, four or five-year old plants. Much larger stocks can be used, but they are more difficult to work with.

Procedure: To begin the operation, saw the plant of the understock off on a slight angle, two to four inches above the ground. Trim the cut surface smooth with a sharp knife and bevel the sides of the stump to allow moisture to drain off. Be sure the edges of the bark are left clean and not jagged. Next, carefully split the stump down the center, being careful not to split it down to the ground. This is done by placing the wide-bladed kitchen knife across the center of the understock and lightly tapping it with the hammer until the cleft is one and one-half to two inches deep. (On very large stocks, two or more splits may be made toward the sides of the stump to accommodate a greater number of scions and to avoid too much pressure.) Once the stock is split, it is ready for actual grafting. Insert the screwdriver down into the center of the cleft to open it wide enough to insert scions on either or both sides. After the cleft is thus opened, select the scion to be grafted and trim it carefully into a wedge. The wedge should be a little thicker on one side than the other. Place the thicker side toward the outside when inserted in the understock. This exerts tension at the point of contact of the cambium layers. This tension usually holds scions securely in place without binding with raffia or rubber bands.

With the scion and understock prepared, the one remaining part of the operation is to join the two together, and this is a crucial point. Actually, the scion is simply a cutting, which is inserted into the root system of another camellia plant, instead of being put into sand to form its own roots. The process of grafting is made possible by the fact that the growth tissues, which provide food for new growth, are contained in the cambium, which is a thin layer of cells between the bark and heartwood. Successful grafting is matching the cambium layer on the understock and scion together, so the two can knit and grow as one.

It is hard for the average person to do this correctly. A good method is to hold a finger on one side of the understock where it is split and press the scion slightly until it feels even with the understock. Then, very slightly, tilt the scion outward so the cambium layer in the scion and in the understock are certain of contact. Where understock is large enough for more than one scion, the chances of success will be increased. Once the scions are wedged into the correct position, gently work the screwdriver free, pull it from the center of the cleft, being careful the scions are not displaced. If the proper size understock is used and the cleft is correctly made, it will not be necessary to tie the graft with string or to use rubber bands. There will be enough pressure to hold scions in place.

Clean all sawdust and mulch from about the graft and saturate the earth around it with Captan or Fermate according to directions on the container. Place a clean wide-mouthed gallon jar over the graft and force gently into the earth. Pack sand around the mouth of jar to seal it. An ordinary paper bag or a burlap sack is put over the jar and weighted down by placing a rock or brick on top of the jar.

The scion may heal over a bit during the next few weeks, but it will not start to grow until new growth starts on other camellia plants in the garden. When the graft has grown near to the top of the jar, it is time to start the hardening-off process. To do this remove sand from around mouth of jar and lift it slightly by placing thin pieces of wood under its lip to admit air from below. After a week or two remove jar entirely and replace with a bean hamper, which will provide shade for the plant until it is thoroughly hardened and will protect the young graft from animals, children and careless gardeners. Remove one slat from the north side of bean hamper when first placed, and as the graft hardens and grows, remove more slats until there is no covering left.

Once the glass jar is removed, the scion will begin an incredibly rapid growth and may reach a height of several feet in the next few months. It will continue a rapid rate of growth until the scion catches up with the root system of the understock. Then the growth will slow down noticeably until the plant will be growing normally.

Thus the propagator will have, in a period of months, a nice plant of a rare new variety or a hard to grow one that would, under other methods of propagation, take years to grow, or much money to obtain from a commercial source.

As soon as glass jar is removed from graft, mulch with pine straw or other good mulching material. Follow the same watering schedule as with other camellia plants in the garden. Most growers do not fertilize the first year after grafting. Sprinkle chlordane or some other good insecticide lightly around plant to discourage insects that might injure tender new growth.

The new graft will bloom in one or two years.

AIR-LAYERING

My favorite method of propagation and one of the simplest is the age-old practice of air-layering. Few materials are required, and if directions are followed, one is reasonably sure of a large, well-branched plant of the same variety as the mother plant within six or seven months. It will perhaps bloom the following season.

The air-layer is made right on the plant soon after the beginning of the growing season, just as the new growth has started to harden. It should not be cut away from the mother plant until a strong root system has developed. This will be about mid-October or November if the air-layer was made in April, as is usual in many parts of America.

Needed to make an air-layer are a sharp knife, a bucket of damp sphagnum moss, plastic wrapping paper or aluminum foil in approximately ten-by-twelve-inch rectangles, and firm string or waxed thread.

Select a healthy, vigorous, symmetrically shaped branch. Any number of air-layers desired may be made on each plant. Branches from one to two feet or even larger may be rooted. After selections are made, proceed as follows: With a sharp knife girdle the branch and cut away a ring of bark about one and one half times the diameter of the branch. After removing bark, scrape away cambium layer (green tissue between bark and wood). Completely cover ringed area with wet, but not soggy, sphagnum moss, which has been soaking in the bucket of water to which hormone rooting powder has been added. The powder can be applied directly to the incision on the limb if desired.

Carefully and snugly draw the covering around the moss, twist firmly at each end and tie securely. It must be tight enough to prevent evaporation and also prevent rain from entering. Should water accumulate inside wrappings during periods of frequent rains, it can be drained away through a few holes pricked in bottom of wrappings. Newly formed roots would be injured by too much moisture. Aluminum foil is an excellent, easy to handle covering, but has the disadvantage of not allowing easy viewing of root structure development. It is necessary to untie and partly unwrap the foil to inspect the roots. If this is done, rewrap and tie again securely. Plastic wrapping will allow easy viewing of root development.

When a good substantial root system has developed, cut off rooted branch from the mother plant just below air-layer. Remove paper foil, but leave moss adhering to roots. Cut off as much of the stump below roots as possible without injuring them. Remove about one-half of the leaves to compensate for shock.

The new plant is now ready for planting. Plant just as any other camellia, being very cautious about not planting too deeply. It will require extra water and shade. If these requirements can be met in the permanent place it is to occupy in the garden, the little plant may be placed directly there, or it may be planted in a pot.

The practice of layering is perhaps the oldest method of plant multiplication with the exception of propagation by seeds. It is a very satisfactory and reliable method of increasing the number of desirable camellias. When plants require heavy pruning, many air-layers may be made as a method of pruning. These plants, attractively potted, make most appreciated gifts.

9

HE FLOWER SHOW

THE HORTICULTURAL DIVISION

Exhibiting camellias is an exciting objective for many growers, offering them an opportunity to test their ability against that of other amateurs. Every exhibitor enjoys winning, of course, but far more satisfying is the knowledge that flower shows are a community service and a means of developing high standards for horticulture.

CUTTING, CONDITIONING, DRESSING, AND TRANSPORTING BLOOMS

1. Cut camellia blooms very early in the morning when they contain the maximum moisture. Select blooms at the peak of perfection—often the best ones are hidden, face down, inside the plant or on low hanging branches. The stem should be one to two inches long; flowers should have one but no more than two leaves.

2. Condition flowers according to the directions given on page 209. Handle gently so as not to bruise the petals.

3. Wipe soiled foliage gently with a soft cloth. If a few black stamens are present, pluck them out with a small pair of tweezers. If blooms are of show quality otherwise, but the edges of one or two petals are damaged by wind, remove the damaged portion carefully with a small pair of sharp scissors.

4. Transport camellias in airtight boxes—the large metal ones designed especially for this purpose are ideal, but any strong, rigid box with a tight cover will do. Cover the bottom of the box with a layer of moss or shredded wax paper (recommended because it does not become soggy). Place the blooms far apart on this layer; spray with a fine mist of water. Cover tightly and store in a cool place until time for the show.

5. Secure entry cards for blooms well before the show and fill out in advance. This will save time and confusion when entering blooms in the show.

6. *Camellia Nomenclature,* published by the Southern California Camellia Society, is recognized as the official nomenclature book by the American Camellia Society. It is published every other year but a variety not included in the book is eligible for show competition.

7. *A Handbook for Camellia Shows,* published by the American Camellia Society, is indispensable for committee member, judge and exhibitor. Like the nomenclature book mentioned above, it may be ordered from the American Camellia Society, Box 465, Tifton, Georgia.

THE SCALE OF POINTS

Point scoring is followed in all camellia shows. This does not mean a literal addition of points for every specimen judged; the scale of points is used to assess the relative importance of the different qualities listed.

Judging in the Horticultural Division is always by American Camellia Society judges, of course.

Plate 18   *A flower show arrangement in an invitational class for a Men's Camellia Club show at Charlotte, North Carolina. Since it was March, I reflected the approaching Easter season with an Italian alabaster Madonna, using harmonious Leucantha camellia flowers and foliage and mahonia and galax leaves.*

Form 20
> (Select a bloom as close to normal as possible for the variety. If the variety has several different forms, select one that is most appealing and most perfect. Any form falling within the description of the bloom as set forth in *Camellia Nomenclature* or known not to be a freak from the judge's experience is deemed typical.)

Size 20
> (It is of course possible for a smaller specimen to score higher on size than a larger specimen of another variety; that is, a big dwarf may score higher than a small giant! Select for exhibit blooms which are large in relation to their potential, except in the case of a miniature, where extra size would disqualify it.)

Color and markings 20
> (Should be clean and bright, within the limits of the variety; judges are aware that weather conditions and soil have decided influence on color. Points are deducted for dull, faded colors; unattractive burns. The only standard for markings is their esthetic appeal.)

Texture and substance 20
> (May be either smooth or crepey, depending on variety. Petals should be lustrous, crisp and firm, with characteristic thickness or thinness. Points are deducted for thin and wilted surfaces.)

Condition and distinctiveness 15
> (Full-blown, fresh flowers. If the variety has stamens, be sure that the anthers are bright yellow and plump, not discolored and limp. Points are deducted if blooms show insect or disease injury, torn petals, discoloration or marks caused by weather bruising or other damage. Distinctiveness is characterized by elegance and perfection.)

XI. *Shishi-Gashira* (C. hiemalis) *with its own foliage and a twisted root in a bamboo container—a free-style Japanese arrangement.*

Foliage 5

> (One or two leaves should remain on each stem. Like the bloom, foliage must be healthy, clean and free from blemishes. The single and semi-double varieties tend to drop blooms, so the American Camellia Society approves the preventative practice of wiring them to their own wood.)

THE ARRANGEMENT DIVISION

Each year a national contest committee composed of expert growers and flower arrangers is appointed by the American Camellia Society. Theirs is the difficult task of preparing flower-show schedules with themes and classes that span the camellia season—November 1 through April 30—and are adaptable to various sections of the country. Their success may be judged by the increasing number of participants and spectators who annually cluster around the Arrangement Division at the camellia shows.

AWARDS

The National Council of State Garden Clubs lists the following awards for shows complying with their standards:

> First, blue ribbon: For best exhibit provided it scores 90 or more points
>
> Second, red ribbon: For next-to-best exhibit scoring 85 or more points
>
> Third, yellow ribbon: Third best provided it scores a minimum of 75 points
>
> Honorable mention, white ribbon: for exhibits which judges deem worthy, regardless of faults
>
> Tricolor, blue-red-and-yellow ribbon: for supreme excellence, to the highest-scoring blue-ribbon winner in a group of classes designated on the schedule; must score at least 95 points.

XII.   *On a bleak winter's day, a greenhouse filled with camellias and their dear companions, azaleas, make a brilliant display for the indoor gardener.* Molly Adams photograph.

All blue-ribbon winners in classes outlined by the Arrangement Committee of the American Camellia Society are eligible for the national contest. Classes added by local committees are not eligible. In addition to special awards and trophies—presented for outstanding arrangements—the American Camellia Society makes the following awards:

> Most outstanding arrangement in contest: Silver trophy to be retained by winner
> Second best in contest: silver trophy to be retained by winner
> First in each class: ACS membership for one year
> Second in each class: Current ACS Yearbook
> Third in each class: Current ACS Yearbook

SCALE OF POINTS FOR CONTEST CLASSES

The scores to be allowed for various qualities of an arrangement are not standard in all shows. They vary according to classes; when local arrangement committees schedule classes in addition to those in the ACS schedule, the scale of points laid down by the National Council for the particular situation is used. The scale of points used in judging the national camellia contest is the following:

Design 35
  (Consideration is given to the six principles of design listed on pages 124-131.)

Interpretation 20
  (Flower show arrangements fall into two broad groups, decorative and interpretive. Decorative arrangements are designed to fill a specific space; period arrangements also fall within this. Interpretive arrangements have story-telling qualities and convey moods, feelings or illusions. Today, most flower show classes are of this type. Interpretive arrangements may be done in one of two ways: either representationally or realistically—to imitate an actual scene and reproduce it in miniature, or by implication and suggestion, to convey the mood, the feeling and the emotion of the artist-arranger. The latter approach is, of course, less obvious and therefore more effective.)

Plate 19 *This beautiful flower show exhibit of a camellia garden was staged by the North Carolina Camellia Society at the Southeastern Flower and Garden Show in Raleigh. Mrs. William P. Kemp, who designed and built it, included statuary from her own garden.* L. P. Watson Studio photo.

Textural values 20
> (Considers whether all the elements, including container,
> accessories and other plant material, are harmonious with
> the camellia.)

Distinction 15
> (Marked superiority of quality, creativity and mechanical
> proficiency. Distinction and originality are scored together,
> but the latter term is often construed to mean spectacular
> or odd, which is of course not the case. The wise arranger
> should think of creativity or self-expression as a synonym
> for originality; only by expressing ourselves are we truly
> unique and therefore original. Unusual combinations of
> plants, unhackneyed designs, color combinations that ex-
> press the mood or season we wish to project—these are the
> methods by which self-expression may be achieved but
> their use should be dictated by our original concept, not
> added self-consciously, like a distracting ruffle on a basic
> black dress. One more point: condition of plant material
> is actually judged under this section.)

Relationship of all material 10
> (Scores the suitability of the materials to each other, to the
> design, use and background.)

—
100

ADDITIONAL CLASSES

There are numerous ways a local arrangement division committee can add interest to this division. Good staging and
lighting are, of course, primary. The simple act of using niches
of different colors, attractively arranged, can relieve monotony
and perk up the show. Special classes can offer scope for the
imagination. Vignettes are always exciting. They may be beautiful segments of any type room with a camellia arrangement
appropriately placed, or, if space is a problem, chests or tables
used with a picture or mirror and an appropriate arrangement
of flowers. In one show, five mantels with arrangements and
accessories formed a charming and unforgettable class.

Hanging arrangements or mobiles, and corsages, well staged,
add interest and variety.

When members of Ikebana International, or other good Japanese flower arrangers are available, they are usually delighted to exhibit in the Japanese manner. Consider staging in tokonomas, on oriental stands, with Japanese hangings or in other suitable ways.

The names of camellias themselves offer inspiration for countless exhibits. What better names for abstract design classes than 'Tomorrow,' 'New Horizons' and 'Fantasy'; or for reception tables 'Pink Champagne' and 'Guest of Honor'; for sophisticated contemporary classes 'Glamour Girl,' 'High Hat' and 'Gay Boy.' For weddings, anniversaries and other romantic occasions consider 'Sweetheart,' 'Cinderella,' 'Keepsake,' 'Melody Lane,' 'Ballet Dancer,' 'Spring Sonnet' or 'First Love.' What better moods to interpet than 'Cheerful,' 'Defiance,' 'Debonair,' 'Mysterious,' 'Admiration,' 'Triumph,' 'Indiscreet,' 'Mischief,' 'Pixie,' 'Modesty,' 'Innocence,' 'Faith' or 'Purity'? There are dozens of camellia names that would serve admirably to salute places, personalities and occasions. Even the places where camellias grow or where there are camellia societies offer intriguing ideas.

NOTES ON TABLE ARRANGEMENTS

Table arrangements always add appeal. If space does not permit dining room tables, a class for patio or other small tables may be used. Exhibitors should study carefully the table section of *The Handbook for Flower Shows*. The decorative unit generally occupies not more than one-third of the length of the table. It need not be centered on the table, of course.

Candles are not used on luncheon tables unless there is an exceptional lack of light. When candles are used, the wicks should be burned. At a seated meal, the flame should be above or below eye level. Test the functionalism of your design by sitting at the table which holds it; vision should be unimpaired.

Accessories used in pairs or singly are attractive on luncheon tables when candles are not used; also, on a buffet table or large refreshment table.

For exhibition purposes, it is not good form to use candies, food, or cut fruits or vegetables which may draw flies.

Schedules usually forbid the use of flat silver and other valuables that may be lost.

Every class in a flower show schedule must be defined in terms that leave no doubt of its meaning in the mind of either exhibitor or judge. While it must be specific, the class must not restrict the imagination nor curb creative expression. Themes and classes should present a challenge and stimulate imagination and creativity. With the whole of creation to serve as a source of inspiration, there will always be room for originality and freshness.

NOTES FOR THE EXHIBITOR

As soon as you are assigned a class and know the space to be filled, assemble the material and begin to experiment. If you are to design for a table, niche, or picture box, duplicate its size at home, and work within that size to achieve proper scale in all aspects. Plant material must not touch the sides of a box nor protrude beyond its limits. Allow a margin between the walls of the box and your design of least 1/12 the height or width of the box. The inside measurement of the standard niche is 42″ high, 28″ wide, 18″ deep, 42″-45″ from the floor.

There is no magic formula that can assure your winning a blue ribbon, but it may help to know that all exhibitors experience similar anxieties in the creative process. Perhaps the stages merge, perhaps they are sharply defined, but the general pattern is as follows:

1. Problem—Something must be done, but how to do it?
2. Incubation—The right answer doesn't come quickly. But the yeast is fermenting and in a few hours, or a few days, will come a burst of inspiration—an idea emerges.
3. Idea—Is it a faint glimmer or the answer to the whole problem? Maybe only a clue.

Plate 20   *At the Southeastern Flower and Garden Show in Charlotte, North Carolina, invitational class, I used a fascinating Aztec ceremonial vase on a teakwood stand above blood-red velvet. The compartment that once held burning sacrifices to the many-faced gods here holds clipped palmetto fronds from a Florida roadsite, Coontie, a palm-like tropical plant, and one White Empress camellia.*

4. Development—You experiment, the interpretation crystallizes, now you can build the design. To continue our yeast analogy, you are ready to bake bread.

5. Critical Revision—You test the bread, and maybe put it back in the oven. That is, you evaluate, refine and perfect the exhibit. Try to "taste" objectively: be sure that your exhibit looks neat and finished in every detail with no mechanical aids visible. (Unless, of course, you are a sophisticated exhibitor in a sophisticated flower show, where modern abstract arrangements are entered. In that case, you will know that the mechanics are very often deliberately left exposed as part of the design structure.)

INVITATION CLASSES

Experienced exhibitors who have won many prizes are often asked to stage flower arrangements as part of the educational process for the public and for novice arrangers. Such invitation classes are sometimes entered in competition, but usually are not. Either way, the schedule should state whether they will be judged.

NOTES FOR THE JUDGE

The marks of the good judge are knowledge, fairness, experience, courage and tact. Flower-show schools are a valuable beginning in qualifying one to evaluate the works of others, but a serious judge must continue to study not only flower arranging, but other forms of art as well, thereby keeping aware of new trends.

The first questions the judge asks when judging an arrangement are: does the arrangement comply with the schedule? does it carry out the theme? (if class is interpretive), or is it suitable for the place and occasion? (if the class is decorative). After these questions are answered to his satisfaction, he proceeds to analyze and evaluate the fine points of the design and the subtleties of the interpretation. He has the ability to employ esthetic principles in his evaluation and cite reasons for his judgment.

The experienced judge submerges his personal preferences and taste and views the arrangements with alert eyes and a clear mind. However, his wide experience enables him to compare the work he is judging with other design experiences; awareness of originality as a factor is thereby heightened.

The good judge never assumes that he is superior to the arranger. Such a judge misses the fresh, new and unusual.

In addition to awarding the ribbons in a flower show, judges are sometimes requested to write comments or criticism on entry cards or other cards provided especially for this purpose. The sensitive and thoughtful judge will not comment on a fault in an arrangement without giving a suggestion for correcting it. Being analytical, he is able to go beyond recording his own feelings. He understands the causes for failure or success, and is able to make the arrangement live for the spectator, helping him understand, appreciate and intelligently enjoy it.

I have long felt that we as flower show judges could be more helpful and make for happy and enthusiastic exhibiting by concentrating our comments on the ribbon winners, pointing out their *merits* along with their faults.

Perfection is never achieved by mere man. When an arrangement is awarded a blue ribbon, it is not implied that it cannot be improved upon. Criticism may be destructive, constructive, complimentary, fault-finding and neutral. The creative art of flower arranging is an interminable thing and the art of judging demands much of us, as critics who verbalize on the artistic expression of others. The flower show judge should be able to communicate his judgment in a clear and interesting manner.

Plate 21 *The footed bronze container is traditional, but the placement of the pandanus leaves suggests modern sculpture because it too makes space a focus. In all design, the spaces or voids are as important as the filled areas. A perfect Leucantha bloom and bud are the plant material.*

10

THE ABC'S OF DESIGN

Landscape design and flower arranging are the only arts in which living line and color are the media of expression, all other arts being founded on inanimate materials. Undoubtedly this offers us both challenge and opportunity. Challenge, because our materials are changing even as we work with them; opportunity, because no artist's palette promises more hope of beauty that that which God provides.

Apart from this initial distinction, all of the arts have more or less fundamental characteristics. These characteristics are balance, contrast, rhythm, scale and proportion, and dominance. By understanding and applying them properly, it is possible for anyone to produce designs with at least some degree of success.

Skill and taste often are equated with good design. We know that skill can be acquired without much difficulty, but taste is more elusive. It varies from country to country, from city to suburb, from decade to decade. To acquire taste, the designer must increase his creative experiences, refine his perceptions, develop his judgment. In so doing, he will learn to distinguish the inherently fine from the merely showy or fashionable. To this end, a knowledge of basic design principles is vital. Let us consider them one by one.

BALANCE

Balance is essential to all art. In a three-dimensional design, balance must be actual as well as visual. The mechanics for making an arrangement that is actually balanced, so that it won't topple over, are covered in another section; here, we deal with visual balance.

Balance may be achieved symmetrically or asymmetrically. In symmetrical balance, plant material of the same visual weight is placed on both sides of the central axis. The material need not be identical, but it must appear to have equal force or weight. Symmetrical balance, which is easy to achieve, is also called static, classical and formal balance. Color Plate X is an example of this type.

Asymmetrical balance is subtler and harder to achieve, but far more alive and exciting. The two opposite sides of the arrangement are not identical, and balance is achieved by placement of material, as well as the material itself. Some of the factors affecting asymmetrical balance are:

> The further from the central axis, the greater the visual force of an object
>
> Bright, fully chromatic colors have more weight than pale tints of colors
>
> Textured surfaces have greater force than smooth ones
>
> Shiny surfaces have more force or pull on the eye than dull ones

Most of the arrangements in this book are balanced asymmetrically.

CONTRAST

Design could not exist without contrast. Two lines crossed at right angles, male and female, rough and smooth, dark and light, dull and bright, curve and straight, yin and yang . . . these exemplify the principle of contrast. Some observations

Plate 22 *In your imagination, continue the long diagonal line of the pine; this becomes the central axis of the design. The gnarled moss-covered limb at the left of the axis is balanced by the Rev. John Drayton camellias and by leaves placed on the central axis or to its right. Solid round forms have more visual force than open linear ones, an important principle to remember when striving for asymmetric balance.*

may be useful to the arranger: in planning a design based on one hue—let's say an all-green or an all-foliage flower arrangement—the lack of color variety must be compensated. That is, strong contrast must be introduced in other elements: perhaps in form, texture, tone, shape or line direction.

To make a color seem stronger, place it next to its complement. Red against green is always more brilliant than red against any other color, as is yellow against violet, and so on around the whole color wheel.

All design elements look stronger, heavier, brighter when seen next to their direct opposites: the vertical line more dramatic against the cross of the horizontal; white is brighter against black. Conversely, to subdue a too-strong contrast, place the troublesome element next to its neighbor, near in color, size, texture, etc.

RHYTHM

Rhythm can be visual as well as audile. In music it is created by a persisting cadence of beats and pauses, a rising and falling of sound. Similarly, in visual composition there is an ordered repetition—of lines, textures, tones, colors and spaces—that satisfy the eye, creating an easy path for it to follow, as it seeks the similar elements to which it is always attracted. I should mention here that "like" does not mean identical. The dark red of Mathotiana camellia may lead to the paler tone of Pink Perfection; the variegated colors of Daikagura camellia may be echoed with the pink form of Daikagura and white snapdragon; the circle of the camellia form may be repeated in the smaller circle of buds and leaves or other flowers.

However this sense of orderly harmony and gradation is accomplished, it is of the essence in attempting to achieve beauty.

In Plate 25, note how rhythm is repetition, the little twiggy lines of pussy willow whirling around the central stem, exemplifying rhythm in Nature. Man-made repetition exists in the curls of the plant material repeating the waves of the container.

Plate 23 *This arrangement tells a little story on our breakfast table. The pompous Italian birds recalled to mind George Eliot's lines about cocks who thought the sun had risen to hear them crow, so I continued the imagery with fronds of dark sago palm to interpret the passing night, and curled one to give a feeling of movement. The white camellia and bud symbolized the coming of light. Note that circles are a recurring rhythm throughout.*

SCALE AND PROPORTION

Books for flower arrangers always list scale and proportion as two distinct fundamentals of composition, but never make plain—at least to me—wherein lies the distinction. I have begun to think of them as a combined principle, rather than as two separate ones. Joined or separated, however, they concern size relationship.

Most of us are able to judge sizes, in fact, we do it all the time, so it is safe to say that we all have a developed sense of size fitness. Nevertheless, it helps to know that one of the first rules of flower arrangement—since relaxed, but still useful for the beginner—required that the longest branch of plant material (the part visible above the container) be at least one and one-half times the height of a vertical container or the width of a horizontal one.

Another point. The components of the design must be related in size. Medium size material can serve as transition between very small and very large flowers, or partly open ones can better relate the size of the fully mature blooms to the buds. Note this application in Plate 27.

One final comment, a rather obvious point but still it is surprising how many designers seem not to consider it. In composing a scene of nature, select all the plants, figures and accessories so they have the same relative size to each other as they would have in the scene they are supposed to represent.

DOMINANCE

The principle of dominance is a fundamental of design. It may be explained in this way: two exactly repeated elements are monotonous, they compete for attention, thereby distracting the eye and creating disunity. However, if one element is subordinated, the other automatically becomes predominant, competition is eliminated, and unity becomes a possibility.

Let us consider how the principle of dominance is applied to form. Think of a square; four lines competing for attention. It is not a very exciting shape. Lengthen the two horizontal lines; the two vertical ones become subordinate, and a hori-

XIII. *A casual arrangement of colorful camellias, with a wicker basket and straw mat to add textural interest.* Hampfler Photo Studio.

XIV. *The gnarled rhododendron root is the catch of a "driftwood fishing" trip in the mountains. Berenice Boddy camellias, aspidistra and leatherleaf fern are the other materials in the Japanese suiban.*

Plate 24 *Perhaps this is a good demonstration of proportion and scale; the branch and container are in a 3:2 ratio, which is a satisfying proportion. To create a natural setting for the Greek figure carrying an amphora, a tall column, reminiscent of Greek architecture, is topped by a branch which could be the shade of a tree. The Florence Stratton camellias are related in color and texture to the figure.*

Plate 25   *To be seen against a wall which had no other decoration, I used a tall branch of forced weeping pussywillow with two umbrella palms and Semidouble Blush camellias. The pussywillow was forced by placing the crushed stem in water in a warm room for three weeks. It dried in this position and decorated a dresser for weeks, but the camellias were replaced as needed.*

zontal rectangle emerges, far more interesting in form than the square. Apply this technique to all the elements of the design—do not use colors, textures, line direction, etc. so that they are evenly divided.

From the attempt to observe this principle came another one of the early rules of arranging: do not use even numbers of flowers. Need I say that this rule is often violated, because sophisticated designers realize that there are many other methods by which dominance may be attained.

FOCALIZATION

Every good design has a focus, an area with a higher degree of interest, which points up the composition as a whole. This area is the climax toward which the rest of the design is built, the place toward which the eye is inevitably drawn. It should seem to grow naturally out of the design. It is here that the major lines of the design converge; here the largest, most colorful, heaviest textures are placed.

If the focal area overpowers the rest of the design, rhythm is destroyed. Over-focalization is often caused by poor grada-tion of form, size, texture, or color, and by too much contrast, by too large a concentration of material. How much contrast or variety is desirable for interest, and how much repetition or likeness for harmony, are questions the arranger must decide. The smaller the quantity of contrasting material, the stronger its quality may be.

Good designs must contain a sense of easy movement from one point of interest to another, and back again through the focus. This is usually accomplished by repetition, gradation and line direction. The focal area should be so integrated with the rhythm of the design that it requires only a momentary pause or rest before the eye moves easily on, without any ,sense of en-trappment.

SPACE AND BACKGROUND

The first consideration when planning an arrangement is the frame, background or space that it will occupy. Most of us have specific areas for designs: a mantel, piano, window, console or table. Ideally, the place chosen should have a plain background to serve as a natural frame against which the arranger can create the desired picture. However, if a patterned drapery or wallpaper are part of the background, you can make a successful design, provided you use heavy foliage to form the silhouette. Lacy small leaves with an open texture will not carry against a pattern. If you are making an arrangement in which camellia foliage is used for the line interest, you will have no problem: it has strong character and will not be lost against any kind of background. Flowers of so many different forms, sizes and colors are available that selecting appropriate ones is relatively easy if you have planted your garden with varieties that fit your needs as a flower arranger.

If there are other accessories, consider them too when making the arrangement. Allow the flowers to dominate, or subordinate them to other ornaments—a wall hanging, book ends, etc. but observe the principle of dominance in your grouping. As in garden design, vertical, horizontal, and mounded shapes compose well together.

To give the arrangement the sense of belonging exactly where it is—this is always a test of good design—try to put it together in the place where it is to be used. In this way, your natural sense of good size relationship will guide you.

TYPES OF ARRANGEMENTS

As in any field, flower arrangers have developed a specialized vocabulary to describe their art. Among the terms in use are:

Line design—Arrangements with distinct silhouettes and contours, as if drawn with pen and ink; they lack shading and mass. Japanese arrangements are linear ones.

Massed designs—Materials used so that they seem to converge, appearing as one unit. Bouquets are an example.

Massed line designs—A distinctively American form, combining linear with massed designs.

Decorative motif—An arrangement having a purely ornamental purpose, the elements of the design so arranged as to create one harmonious whole.

Plate 26   *When the units of a design are harmonious in size, color and feeling, they mix well. The black pottery container and dracaena leaves, well suited in size, have a rather masculine force; the pink in the leaves blends with the pink hues of camellia varieties Debutante, Marchioness of Exeter and Berenice Boddy.*

Plate 27   *The alabaster figure and the floral design have a unifying theme—triangles are dominant. Note how the three-sided shapes recur, even in the pointed chin of the boy. I reinforced the theme with a trinity of camellia leaves and blossoms, held in two white shells which are associated—by imagination and visually—to the young fisherman. Camellias used are Yuki-Botan and White Queen.*

Plate 28   *Contrast, an important design principle, is apparent here. Strong white (painted sea fans); against black (sprayed dried papyrus, container and base); contrast of line direction (elongated slender verticals against solid horizontals) and contrast of textures (laciness against density and smooth against rough). I made this arrangement in a lecture-demonstration for a Ikebana International Chapter. While I would never use this arrangement in a traditional setting it was effective for demonstration work and would be also effective in certain modern settings.*

Plate 29 *Hosta forms the background for this arrangement, its lovely foli-age arching over the camellias and bits of fern to better relate all the design elements (in the same way that weeping forms of trees relate the sky to the earth. The drooping moss in Plate 3 accomplishes the same purpose). The sasanqua camellias are charming in flower arrangements though most varie-ties shatter very quickly.*

Plate 30 *Designed for a buffet table at our river cabin, this contemporary arrangement in an old English wooden bowl holds camellias, azalea, and aspidistra. It would be quite at home in any room with a country feeling.*

Expressive or interpretive motif—An arrangement which reproduces or symbolizes with flowers and figures (if desired) a mood, thought, feeling, character, scene, etc.

Modern abstract motif—A new style of arrangement which fragments or abstracts its original subject. The beholder is meant to view it as a form and color combination . . . "as a representation of *mood* and not as a representation of objects", in the words Kandinsky used to describe his paintings. Designs of this kind are hard to relate to traditional ones, requiring no focus, area of interest, etc. They do, however, challenge the imagination, are strongly interpretative, and often create an effect of fantasy.

Elements of design—The separate ingredients or details in any plan, which can be analyzed. The ingredients are line, form, pattern, texture, and color.

Conclusion: Study the principles of design as applied to all man-made art. Practice, and a love and understanding of nature, will guide you to combine flowers and plant materials as a painter paints a picture, or as a composer writes music. In this way you will express the inner spirit. Art grows out of nature and enriches life. A flower arrangement, in addition to adorning the home, can suggest the grandeur and power of nature.

11

TYLES AND PERIODS
IN FLOWER ARRANGEMENT

Flower arrangement today is a blend of many periods and many lands. "Period" arrangements were developed in different European countries in different eras. They are not based on any set rules of design, but are enjoyed for their well-ordered abundance and lavish color. In America, this blend of periods and places has taken expression in the art form known as the massed-line flower arrangement. In Japan, on the other hand, the emphasis of the composition is on line, mass playing only a minor role.

BORROWING FROM THE PAST

Good things from many periods and many countries may be used together in perfect harmony and with easy grace. Only when periods are too far apart in essentials, such as scale, line, color and texture, are they inharmonious. Always adhere to the basic elements of good design and good taste in mixing eras.

Man's search for beauty in his own past can be a never-ending pleasure. Borrow from the past; be inspired and stimulated by it; use it as a foundation on which to build, and as a guide to your own self-expression.

Against the simple lines of contemporary furniture and textured surfaces, antique and Old World accents glow with a warmth that only long tradition can give. A beautiful old piece of art, or a beautiful arrangement of flowers in a vase, can transform a trite interior into a scene of interest. The camellia, in its many forms, is versatile in creating the feeling of any era. It is effective in bountiful period bouquets, in sculptured contemporary styles and in linear Oriental arrangements.

INFLUENCE OF VARIOUS PERIODS

A knowledge of periods is as important to the modernist as to the traditionalist, since the present can best be seen against the background of the past. This knowledge is a prerequisite to mixing periods and styles with success.

Flowers are a part of living and always have been. Naturally they have been used in the styles, forms and colors that parallel other decorations of the particular period. There are flower arrangements typical of Early American use, Victorian, French, 18th Century English, Colonial Williamsburg, etc. To learn more about these different styles, one has only to examine authentic fabrics, paintings and other period art objects. Briefly, however, let us summarize the various periods and work in the region where camellias are heavily planted— Camellia Country.

EARLY AMERICAN: Primitive designs in crude containers of rough-hewn wood, pewter, copper, brass, ironstone or crockery—with no apparent floral design. Camellias with fruit would make a lovely informal Thanksgiving design for a home decorated in the Early American manner.

ANTE-BELLUM: Luxurious floral arrangements with garlands of camellias decorating the house. Strong French and Spanish influences. French porcelain, crystal epergnes, alabaster urns are authentic containers. For an informal design, try a low porcelain basket.

VICTORIAN: Tussy-mussies, containers stuffed to the brim with flowers. Arrange waxed camellias with a variety of blooms

Plate 31 *French in feeling, an antique silver basket suitable for ante-bellum rooms and other elegant interiors holds the dependable old variety Prince Eugene Napoleon arranged here with one of my favorite companion plants, elaeagnus.*

Plate 32   *Regency, Directoire and Empire decorating styles were strongly influenced by classic design. Here a classical placement of aspidistra leaves forms the background for the Greek figure with two Governor Earl Warren camellias to contribute striking color. This arrangement was used on one end of a spinet piano.*

under a glass dome for a very special effect. Tiffany glass vases, too, are perfect foils for velvety camellias.

18TH CENTURY GEORGIAN AND COLONIAL: The arrangements at Colonial Williamsburg offer many inspired ideas for the use of camellias. Bouquets arranged in an equilateral triangle, oval, or fan pattern are appropriate. Many of the classic containers of the period, such as pitchers, bowls or cornucopias, are available today in excellent reproductions.

FRENCH: Containers of marble and alabaster, urns of gilt and bronze, figurines of Dresden or Bisque—all these are typical of Directoire, and all mix well with the waxy quality of the flowers of the camellia.

SPANISH: With the increased popularity of Spanish décor today, it is very likely that there will be a heightening of interest in Spanish floral art. In the Western Hemisphere, the Spanish influence is evident in the art of South America, the American Southwest and Far West. These are all areas in which camellias flourish.

For Spanish designs, consider brilliant colors, lush tropical leafage, and desert cacti and succulents to use as camellia companions. Wrought iron, tile and clay containers ranging from the very primitive to the very elegant—Moorish brass, carved wood, even papier mâché lacquered to a porcelain finish—are in keeping with this style.

CONTEMPORARY AMERICAN: A blend of many different styles, reflecting the heterogeneous American tastes in furniture and room décor and our wide travels throughout the world. Flower arrangements are massed-line in design. Containers are most often the unexpected; sometimes severely modern in design, more often borrowed from another period or perhaps from another country.

MODERN: Modern art has had tremendous impact on advanced flower arranging, particularly for exhibition work in flower shows. Modern abstract designs are defined on page 137 Emphasis is on architectural type of design, with mechanics frequently exposed, rather than concealed as in other arrangement styles.

JAPANESE: Japanese is probably the most popular of all flower arrangement styles in use today, so I have devoted the following chapter to it.

Plate 33 *In a rustic river cabin, the panelled wall is a background for grey driftwood, hosta and camellia foliage; white camellias with yellow stamens and tiny yellow flowers of the sassafras made a pleasing color harmony. The sassafras was forced into early bloom indoors.*

XV.   One bloom and bud of Daikagura camellia, two cattails, two aspidistra leaves, and a feathery evergreen, form a modern Japanese design in
a modern grey container on a plain base.

XVI. A naturalistic moribana arrangement combines nandina, sasanqua camellias, ferns and grasses as they grow in my garden. A clump of small yellow mums add color. The stones which hide the needlepoint holders were rubbed smooth by a tumbling mountain stream. (My grandchildren think it is fun to have a "Mimi" who collects sticks and stones!)

Plate 34　*In the manner of Colonial Williamsburg a tall silver container from England holds waxed fruit and Debutante camellia designed for a dining-room table. A circle of balsam with more fruit and camellias and silver candlesticks with white tapers complete the decorative unit.*

Plate 35 *Where elegance is appropriate, the silver balance makes a charming floral container for a luncheon or dinner table. I sometimes use a round mirror base instead of this carved wooden one. Pink snapdragons are used here with Pink Perfection and Lallarook camellias. Small needlepoint holders secure the arrangement.*

Plate 36 *The old and the new are companionable when essentails such as mass, line, color and texture are considered. Here an ancient bronze vase harmonizes with the deep-red of variegated banana leaves and Aunt Jetty camellia. The arrangement placed against a blue wall in my eighteenth century living room added spice to the room.*

Plate 37 *Whaleback palm leaves from my mother's garden in Florida and White Empress camellias with their own foliage form a bold contemporary design which is strong in contrasts. The coarse ribs of the palm and the heavy texture of the black iron compote emphasize the pale fragility of the camellias. The needlepoint holder is hidden by clinkers sprayed with flat black paint.*

$\mathcal{J}$APANESE FLOWER ARRANGEMENT

It is a delight to speculate on the role of the camellia in flower arrangement, both camellias and floral art having had their origin in the Orient. No doubt the camellia was one of the first flowers to be arranged, centuries ago, for the altar; since they symbolize longevity and good fortune, camellias have long been intimately associated with Japanese customs and traditions.

Flower arranging—founded by men and still considered a manly art in the Orient—was developed concurrently with the spread of Buddhism into Japan. At the beginning, it was practiced only by temple priests, but interest grew and by the fifteenth century, arranging flowers was permanent home art. This was true to such an extent that a special niche for flowers, the tokonoma, was prominent in most Japanese homes.

Many schools were established, each teaching different rules, techniques and symbolism. However, the differences between schools were seldom major, but often they involved only the names applied to the main line, a slight change in measurement, or a different meaning attributed to the plant material.

Plate 38 *Classical Japanese Arrangement. The formal Japanese usabata holds forced branches of pussywillow for the shin (heaven) and soe (man) groups. The (tai) earth group is a neijime of Pink Perfection camellias. The stems are placed close together in a kubari, or forked stick, which is placed taut in the container. Another stick called akomi wedges the stems firmly in the crotch of the kubari.*

Flower arranging schools still play a prominent part in Japanese life, and it is not unusual to find some which teach classical arrangement exactly as they did centuries ago. However, since Japan opened its doors to the western world, western influences have been at work. As a result, arrangements have become less restrained, less rigidly controlled. Modern designs are popular, some of them free style, others still following classic principles.

From the hundreds of schools come three major groups of styles of interest to Americans: Classical or Traditional, Nageire, and Moribana.

CLASSICAL

Classical or traditional styles have unyielding rules and measurements. Hardest of all to make, they require considerable study before mastery of their construction is possible. Arrangements requiring so specialized a study are not practical for our purposes, nor is the knowledge of the traditional symbolism, which is an integral part of these arrangements. However, the study of rules governing the construction of classical arrangements will help us gain knowledge that can be applied to making any type of arrangement, whether it is the informal Japanese arrangement, the American interpretation of line called massed-line arrangement, the mass arrangement or the free interpretation.

Instead of a needlepoint holder, a forked twig, called a kubari, is placed taut in a classical container, with the apex of the triangle toward the arranger. All stems are placed within the fork and wedged firmly in the crotch of the kubari with another stick, called a komi. When finished, a classical arrangement must emerge from the container like a single stalk. The stalk must be free of any small branches, leaves, or flowers for about three and one half inches above the neck of the container.

NAGEIRE

The Nageire is an unstudied, natural arrangement of plant material in a tall container. The word nageire means "to throw in", giving the impression that the plant material is simply or carelessly tossed into the container. This is far from the truth. Each branch, each flower, and each container presents an individual problem and requires different handling. Usually, when the main branches are securely anchored, the others can be easily balanced in the design. Nageire arrangements are classified into three groups: upright, incline, and cascade or flowing. There are many variations to the basic patterns, one school listing thirty. This offers infinite possibilities and patterns to follow.

A charming story is connected with the origin of the Nageire style. During the fifteenth century, an outstanding tea ceremony master accompanied the great Japanese general Hideyoshi to the battlefield. One hot day, by mutual consent, the opposing armies paused so that their generals could enjoy a cup of tea. General Hideyoshi ordered his tea ceremony master to arrange some iris which were growing nearby. The tea master picked the iris, grouping a few leaves around them. Then piercing the stems with the blade of his dagger, he tossed the group into a waterbucket, which had been placed near the general in a crude attempt at air conditioning. The arrangement stood upright in the bucket and the general, impressed with its design cried, "What a beautiful throw-in arrangement". From that day Nageire, or flowers apparently thrown into a tall container, became a part of the tea ceremony and grew in popularity.

MORIBANA

Moribana, meaning "piled up flowers" style was originated about the beginning of the twentieth century. An informal style, it is constructed in a low, flat container and the plant material is inserted in a needlepoint holder. This is the easiest of all

Plate 39   *Japanese Sanshu-ike, or a Shoka Arrangement of Three Materials. Clipped palmetto palm which grows in wild abundance in the deep south and can be purchased at the florist in the north, aspidistra, and Leucantha camellias are the three materials in the black Japanese compote.*

Plate 40   *Another Sanshu-ike arrangement. Here bird of para-dise flowers, birds of paradise foliage, and Leucantha camellias are used in a modern blue ceramic container. As you will observe from the frequency with which I have used this variety of ca-mellia, it is one of my favorites. The Japanese generally prefer single or semi-double camellias. They believe that stamens and pistils are more important than petals, just as the heart of man is more important than his flesh.*

styles to learn, and with a little practice the basic patterns can be created. There are a number of variations to the basic patterns. Moribana, originated to meet the need for an arrangement to be viewed from more than one side, is the most practical of the Japanese styles for American homes.

All Japanese arrangements are based on three main lines, which represent the three great parts of the universe—heaven, man and earth. Heaven is dominant; man is second, and earth is last. There may be other lines to strengthen the three main lines, but the assisting lines must not be any longer or more dominant than the line they assist. These lines, or groups of lines, have definite relationships to each other. The length of the main heaven stem or line sets the scale for the whole arrangement. Its length depends on the size of the container, the space where the arrangement is to be placed, and type of material. All other lines are in proportion to this main line and grouped about it. Stem lengths vary according to styles and schools. Generally, heaven is one and one-half to five times the height of a tall container or width of a flat container. Man is two-thirds to three-fourths of heaven, and earth is usually one-third of heaven, or one-half to three-fourths of man.

Japanese arrangements are particularly well suited to camellias, the linear designs showing off the loveliness of each bloom. Ikebana, the word for Japanese flower arrangement, appeals to people who enjoy a few flowers rather than great masses; it makes possible arrangements of natural flowing beauty with one flower and some companion foliage.

Mastering Japanese arrangement is a life's work. However, the person who has neither the time nor inclination to delve into the subject may well concentrate on the technique of making even one of the basic forms, using it as a pattern for creating a wide variety of lovely arrangements.

Study of Japanese flower arrangement will develop a sensitiveness to line, proportion, balance, and rhythm. Memorize the proportions of plant material to the container, the proportions and direction of the lines of the three main groups and use this knowledge to create flower arrangements of beauty, distinction, and originality.

Plate 41 *Pine roots are the line interest in this modern Japanese arrangement made for a window ledge in my husband's office. The tip of a pine branch and one camellia (Elizabeth Boardman) were the fresh plant material. The flower was replaced as needed by other varieties and colors. The pine roots are simply laid on top of the container, and the pine branch and camellia fitted easily inside without any mechanics.*

Plate 42 *Grey lichen-covered wild plum branch inspired this Nageire arrangement in my favorite tall black container. The branch needed little pruning and fitted securely into the container without any mechanics. Small protruding nubs provided apertures for the branch of Macrantha azalea and Berenice Boddy camellias. I used this on a television cabinet against a blue wall.*

Plate 43 *Particularly with pine, it is seldom we find a branch that can be used without pruning. I ruin many branches in trimming them. This one was quite large before clipping. To achieve the desired angle the branch was wired to a straight stick a little shorter than the height of the container, and that stick was impaled on a needle-point holder in the bottom of the vase. The stems of the Tricolor (Siebold) camellias were lengthened enough to bring them to the desired height by wiring them to sticks also. The pine made a practical design which lasted for weeks. Fresh flowers were added as needed.*

Plate 44   *Mr. Sofu Teshigahara, headmaster of the Sogetsu School of Japa-*
nese flower arranging, considers the camellia a perfect flower for in itself it
combines the basic elements of art—line, form, texture and color. I agree!
     In this Japanese arrangement made for a lecture-demonstration I have
used an elm branch covered with grey moss in a grey pottery container.
Small pine branches are fillers and background for the Martha Brice ca-
mellias.

Plate 45 *Japanese Moribana arrangement. The boat is carved from a solid piece of wood with only a small copper-lined recess for needlepoint holder, water, and plant material. The upward thrust of the pineapple leaves broken by the diagonal of the bent leaf gives a feeling of the motion of a sail. Umbrella palm and a Catherine Cathcart camellia with its own foliage complete the design. A bamboo raft is the base. I made this arrangement for a lecture demonstration at the South Atlantic Regional Garden Club Meeting.*

13

FOR SPECIAL OCCASIONS AND PLACES

Decorating for winter holidays is no problem for the arranger who has camellias blooming in the garden. Then, in an otherwise barren season, our joy in seeing this aristocratic shrub in flower is unconfined! With one or two blooms and a sprig of green, it is possible to arrange table centerpieces, (Plate 62), Christmas decorations (Plates 47 through 54), and other ornaments appropriate to the season, place and occasion.

CAMELLIAS AT THE ALTAR

Painting, sculpture, architecture—indeed all the arts—developed from man's need to express his inner self and to give spiritual meaning to the physical world around him. Since man was created in a garden, it is probable that his first votive offering was a blossom. We do know that the custom of placing flowers upon the altar of worship dates back to pagan times. Not until the sixth century A.D., however, was a formal floral art developed, supposedly in Japan as a result of the spread of Buddhism from China. The rules were complex, each stem and flower positioned with mathematical exactness according to a rigid symbolism.

Plate 46   *A Moribana arrangement made for a book shelf in the Public Librbary is designed with branches of cope tree, and one bloom and one bud of George B. Barrett camellia in a grey pottery container. The needle-point holder is covered with small grey stones.*

These old rules have little application to the needs of today's arrangers, even in contemporary Japan. But the spirituality and the sensitivity to place and occasion with which these early religious arrangements were made should be continued by members of contemporary altar committees.

Camellia flowers have been little used in our churches, but their dignity, their large, striking shape which is easily seen from the distance, and their longevity, make them most appropriate. Blooming in the bleakness of winter, they remind the congregation that however severe the weather, everlasting life surges forth from the earth.

It is seldom that the arranger can cut camellia branches that are as long as church designs require. Therefore other foliage becomes necessary. Shrubs whose branches make a good structural background are sasanqua, ligustrum, cherry laurel, elaeagnus and holly. Well-conditioned blooms may be carefully wired to the selected branches, following the procedure for corsages. The flowers should be handled gently, of course; they bruise easily. Also good with camellias are the leaves of aspidistra, canna, large hosta, and palm fronds.

Spikes of gladiolius, snapdragon, and stock, all available from the florist, have a rather formal quality which makes them particularly suitable for church use. They combine well with the camellia blossoms, the contrasted shapes adding interest and variety to the design.

The container should reinforce the suggestion of dignity in the architecture of the church, and the design should subordinate itself to the solemnity of the place and occasion. It must never distract, existing only as a grace note in the religious scene.

Living as we are in a modern world and a fast tempo, the God-given qualities of heart and soul are often neglected. Therefore it is doubly important that we develop inner reserves of strength and composure. Working with plants helps this spiritual development.

The affinity between the worshipper and the artist is deep, for in commiting oneself to a larger purpose—the real values,

Plate 47   *The beautifully carved Madonna forms the dominant line of this Christmas arrangement made for one end of the spinet piano. I chose white gladioli, green dracaena leaves, and two kinds of white camellias, September Morn and Joshua E. Youtz, because their elegance and dignity were comparable to the fineness of the figure.*

let us say—there is no room for the frustrations of everyday living to take root. How fortunate, therefore, is the arranger who has the opportunity to use flowers not only to give glory to God, but also to express her own creative impulse.

WAXED CAMELLIAS

While flowers are always more beautiful in their natural state, camellias treated with paraffin wax become like porcelain. Flowers so treated last several days longer than their normal life span, and can be easily shipped by packing in shredded paper.

Single and loose, fluffy, semi-double varieties in pink, rose and white are suited to waxing. The formal doubles, rose form doubles and peony and anemone forms with tight centers do not lend themselves to this treatment. The darker blooms are not as pretty when waxed as are the white and pastel ones. Choose fresh blooms, free of imperfections. Remove any ants that may have congregated in the center by gently blowing on it, or flick off with a tiny brush.

To wax camellias, melt four or five pounds of wax in the top part of a three-quart double boiler to which a candy thermometer has been hooked. After wax is melted, remove from fire to cool. When the temperature has dropped to 145° dipping may begin. Holding them by the stem submerge one bloom at a time, very briefly, in the wax, giving it a quick twirl to be sure all petals are completely covered. Be sure bloom does not touch sides or bottom of pan. Dip the waxed bloom immediately into a large pan of ice water. Be careful that the bloom is gently submerged in the ice water, because the petals will "set" as they hit the water. Let the blooms float for ten or fifteen minutes and then turn upside down on a thick towel to dry.

As the wax in the double boiler cools and a skim forms on top, replace the pan over the boiling water and bring the temperature again to 145° F. before continuing to dip.

Waxed camellias are too heavy to use for corsages, but can

Plate 48   *For a Christmas doorway: a balsam and boxwood wreath, green satin bow and Lady Clare camellias. The camellias were wired to florist picks and inserted into the straw form of the wreath. The damp, cool out-of-doors kept flowers lovely for several days but as they faded, they were replaced with fresh ones.*

Plate 49 *Mother and child are represented by the graceful sculpture and also symbolized by the bloom and bud of Magnoliaeflora camellia. A pincup holder concealed behind the folds of the skirt holds the camellias and sago palm fronds.*

be wired to florist picks or sturdy stems for use in flower arrangements. They are quite lovely displayed flat on a silver or crystal tray, and are also attractive with waxed fruit, to make a long-lasting arrangement for a holiday table. To wax fruit, proceed just as for waxing camellias, but melt two white crayons into the wax to give a lovely translucence. Fruit can withstand a higher temperature than flowers.

PACKING AND SHIPPING CAMELLIAS

The best way to enjoy camellias is to share them with others. Give them away, wear them, and display them to advantage in the garden, in flower arrangements and in shows. Perhaps the blooms enjoyed most are those shipped to friends in cold regions where they seldom have a camellia bloom. If properly prepared and handled, flowers can be shipped to far distant places and arrive garden-fresh and unbruised.

Shipping Corsages: See page 216 for the most satisfactory method of preparing the flowers. The flowers so prepared are ready for packing. It is best to pack each flower in an individual box. A box should be about four or five inches in diameter with a hole in the center. Run the wire stem of the flower through the bottom of the box and bring part way up the side of the box. This will hold the bloom firmly and assure safe travel. Be sure the petals are free from the sides of box.

The secret of maintaining the crisp quality of the bloom is to keep it as nearly airtight as possible. Therefore, after spraying the flower lightly with water, cover the box with one of the plastic papers such as Saran wrap or Handi-wrap and seal with tape. Pack these individual boxes in a good substantial corrugated box of proper size to hold the number of blooms to be shipped. The recipient of the blooms can use one flower at a time, putting the others in the refrigerator and thus enjoy them for many days.

For Flower Arrangements: To ship blooms for use in arrangements, select fresh open flowers and a few buds of varying degrees of development. Be sure all have good stems if possible. Pass florist wire through the blooms and twist the wire carefully and inconspicuously down the stem of each.

Obtain a regular florist shipping box if available, but any strong, shallow box will do. It should be shallow, but not so shallow that the lid will touch the flowers. Cut a piece of cardboard to fit snugly as a false bottom. Place each bloom on the false bottom and wire the stem firmly to it. The flowers must be placed so they do not touch each other or the sides of the box. Then firmly secure the false bottom with flowers attached in the shipping box. Spray with a light mist of water from an atomizer, seal the box tightly and wrap securely. Mark the box "Rush, Cut Flowers, Perishable" and ship by the quickest means.

There is no need to place moss, paper, cotton or any other packing around, under or over blooms. Such materials work loose in transit and bruise the flowers.

Plate 50   *The shape of the modern grey pottery Madonna, designed by Mr. Gregory Conway, inspired this Christmas arrangement for my mantel. Aspidistra dramatically emphasizes the form of the figure, and a hosta leaf carries the line to a satisfactory finish, gracefully relating the composition to two black scroll bases. Delicate pink Debutante camellias are lovely against the grey of the Madonna.*

Plate 51 *A circle, symbolizing a halo, is formed by gold-sprayed aspidistra leaves framing the gold-mantled Italian Madonna of singular sculptural qualities. The long ascending line is composed of two dried papyrus, also gilded. A Purity camellia, placed off-center, accents the Madonna which is framed by feathery evergreen to create a feeling of mystical unreality. A simple black base completes the composition.*

Plate 52 *The tranquil form of this too-popular ceramic Madona is used here in an unusual manner for a Christmas design for my desk. One white sea-fan is attached to the white painted palm spathe container with florist clay. I placed one beautiful Purity camellia at the feet of the Madonna as a gift to the Child whose birth we celebrate.*

Plate 53 *My favorite Christmas figure, an Italian alabaster Madonna with the Christ Child, is used here in an arrangement for a living-room table. An antique brass candelabrum with three white candles provides height. The plant material, impaled in a hidden pincup holder, is juniper, Arum itallicum, and Joshua E. Youtz camellias. The Bible is open at the Christmas Story.*

Plate 54   *Madonnas need not be expensive to be beautiful and effective in arrangements. This large, gracefully designed one is of inexpensive white pottery. Here it is used with aspidistra and Mathotiana camellias for a holiday arrangement on a chest. It is charming also with white camellias at Easter.*

Plate 55   *"To Sundry Notes of Music", an interpretation of Shakespeare's sonnets. The graceful Mexican wood carving suggested the theme and the design. Plant material which is placed in a cup-holder includes banana leaves, green dracaena foliage, and White Empress camellias with their own foliage. The scrolled stand is a harmonious choice; a second small stand under the figure gives added height and prevents a feeling of heaviness at the bottom.*

Plate 56   *A Camellia Christmas Tree. Gold-sprayed Japanese paper umbrellas in graduated sizes on a dowel form an unusual Christmas decoration which I have used in varied ways. The stand is hidden wtih boxwood clippings, and later small gift packages are heaped at the base. Camellias in hues of pink and red were placed in orchid tubes and Scotch-taped to the umbrellas in groups of three. Varieties used are Pink Perfection, Mathotiana, Rose Dawn and Lallarook. The crystal drops contributed to the effectiveness of the design.*

Plate 57 *Wedding Cake. Soft pink Papaver (sasanqua) camellias surround the revolving silver tray which holds the white wedding cake. The camellias on the cake are made of sugar icing and are exact copies of the real blooms surrounding it.* Photographed by Ennis Atkins.

Plate 58   *To toast the New Year, a brandy snifter with a burning white candle (anchored with a bit of florist clay) on a small Japanese burl, sets the stage for a procession of camellia blooms. Here a variegated Daikagura and bud were anchored on a very tiny pinpoint holder. Occasional misting with water was all that was necessary to keep blooms fresh and turgid for several days.*

Plate 59   *Golden pheasants combined with golden cornucopias from which spill waxed fruit, ivy and Dawn (C. vernalis) camellias centered our family Thanksgiving table. I sometimes use brass candlesticks with this combination.*

Plate 60 *The hobbies of gardening and flower arranging lead down many bypaths. Those of us who love Madonnas for Christmas usually find ourselves with a collection. This one, beautifully carved in Mexico, is placed here on the piano with brass angel candleholders, also from Mexico. The camellias are Joshua E. Youtz. Unity of the various elements is achieved by their placement on a well-proportioned burl. I like the voids in this composition too.*

Plate 61 *The white porcelain figures and vases from Italy can be arranged in many ways for effective and easy-to-do table decorations. Here they are on a buffet table. Yucca spikes and boxwood are the foliages and the camellia is Joshua E. Youtz.*

Plate 62   *An antique silver container which we found in Madrid is ideal for the dining-room table. Here it is arranged wth fruit accented by a large Elizabeth Boardman camellia placed on front and back of the arrangement to make it free-standing, that is, completed on all sides.*

Plate 63 *A modern Valentine designed for a February meeting of my Garden Club. Yucca forms a strong vertical line to which sago palm is fastened with Scotch tape to fashion a heart. Prince Eugene Napoleon camellias are used here, but Professor Charles S. Sargent is also a fine Valentine camellia.*

Plate 64   *The similar color and textural quality of the shells and the White Queen camellia suggested that they be used in combination. Hosta leaves provide pleasing contrast, and a green linen cloth furnished a suitable background. The plant material was impaled in a tiny pincup holder.*

*A*CCESSORIES, CONTAINERS, AND BASES

Flower arrangements, fragile and transitory though they are, provide one of the chief means of expression for many of us. We use our garden gifts not only for home decoration, but also to express our inner feelings and moods. Consequently, arrangers like to stage designs to tell a story, to harmonize with a period setting, or possibly to interpret a holiday. Objects of art, whether shaped by man or nature, are tremendously useful for this purpose, if selected in colors, textures, shapes, and sizes that will carry out the idea.

No matter what you use, a chunk of rock or a priceless sculpture, be sure that it emerges as an integral part of the over-all plan. It may be subordinate to or dominant over the flowers, but it should be necessary in some way to the picture you are creating. If the design is just as effective without it, the accessory is, at least in this particular instance, useless.

If you are simulating a scene from nature, select pieces which are in scale; the figure leaning against a branch which represents a tree must have the same relative size as man has to a real tree. This does not mean that you pull out a tape measure. Interpretive flower arrangement is an abstract art;

it is more successful if it plays on the imagination of the beholder rather than makes faithful representations. But the point is to make your viewer believe that your scene could be real.

Reality can be many things. Plato first formulated the doctrine that what we conceive is as real as physical substance. For me, the reality of traveling is a recurring experience through my flower arrangements. As I tuck a few flowers into the jug from Egypt, arrange camellias around a figure from Mexico, or create a line around alabaster from Rome, I recreate the pleasures of earlier voyages. Of course, with this sound logic I easily convince myself (and Paul) that the souvenir on which I may have set my heart is an economy rather than a luxury!

Many times the object is free for the taking. In the natural world around us handsome articles lay concealed, awaiting only the eye of some perceptive arranger. Weathered wood, barren tree roots, rocks and shells—here is a wealth of dramatic material, frequently overlooked, perhaps because it comes without a price tag. If one can't see beauty in the simple things of life that are free, it is not likely he can recognize beauty when it is for sale.

To make truly distinguished designs, the seeing eye must be developed. With increasing awareness of the things around us, plant material is no longer only a flower or a branch, but an ingredient having line, form, color, and shape with which to create a composition.

DRIFTWOOD

The beaches, lake shores and forests yield interesting abstractions of wood and roots, moss and bark, shaped by nature— some as dynamic as sculpture by Jacob Epstein. These marvelously textured materials are superb contrasts for the smoothness of the camellia blossom. Use them to establish a lovely line for the arrangement, or subordinate them to the pattern selected for the flowers. Driftwood and bark make good flower

Plate 65   *The unusual old carved bamboo container from Japan holds a spring arrangement of one forced branch of gum tree, pink tulips, tulip foliage, and the beautiful pink Martha Brice camellia which is just the color of the tulips.*

containers as well, and small pieces are ideal for hiding the mechanics of the design.

A basic book on the subject, the *ABC of Driftwood for Flower Arrangers* by Florence M. Schaffer (Hearthside Press, Inc., New York), tells how to prepare nature's bounty. Roots and wood often can be broken off or sawed into the desired shape. If the wood is very dirty, it should be scrubbed with steel wool or a brush. Then any of the furniture-finishing techniques can be applied: sanding; bleaching in Clorox; staining to match a table of mahogany, walnut or other wood; waxing; polishing; and even painting with a flat paint or water color to harmonize with the setting.

Generally, driftwood is at home in family rooms, dens, seaside houses or mountain cabins. However, a beautifully smooth and elegant piece, which has been polished by nature or sand blasted, may be used as the dominant line in a formal arrangement. Many pieces are dramatically effective in modern homes, but weathered wood should not be used on highly polished tables unless it is first refinished as suggested in the preceding paragraph. Of course, you will want to use a base or stand to avoid damage to fine furniture if the water seeps out.

SHELLS

Artists through the ages have drawn inspiration from the sea, which is a rich and an inexhaustible source of intricate patterns, textures, shapes, and colors. Shells may be used as vases, as centers of interest, or simply as devices to conceal the paucity of flowers. Texturally their translucence makes them an ideal accompaniment for camellias.

ROCKS

The grouping of stones to form a design apparently stems from the rockery, a centuries-old feature of oriental gardens. In fact, the Japanese often use weathered stones even without plant

Plate 66   *The Aztec bowl is quite compatible as a container for a Japanese arrangement of dried hydrangea, aspidistra and Marjorie Magnificent camellias. The black lacquered bases edged in Chinese red, the reddish-brown of the container, and the pink of the hydrangea and camellia, make a quite pleasing color effect.*

material as outdoor decoration. In China, stones sculptured by nature are so greatly prized that they are handed down as precious family heirlooms. The quality of rocks is determined by their varying hues, texture, grain and degree of translucence. Stones confer a quality of permanence and solidity to any floral design. Rocks serve another purpose. Since they are available in varied sizes and shapes, they provide a means of transition and also repetition of design elements.

Rocks help create contrast, depth, background and focal points. Slate and other flat rocks are useful bases and potential containers if the flowers are secured in a pinholder. To conceal the mechanics, small stones may be placed around the holder. Large, irregular stones may suggest mountains or other aspects of nature in a landscape composition. Do not overlook the commercial stone yard as a source of rocks for special effects. Lava, cinders, and glass chips are also useful to the arranger.

PLUMES AND PEACOCK FEATHERS

Large plumes may be used to create unusual effects in flower arrangement. The large, brilliantly colored tail feather of the peacock, with a prominent "eye", is very decorative. In imperial China, peacock feathers were the insignia of high officials, conferred by the emperor as a reward of merit, to be worn on the hat. The peacock has traditionally been a symbol of splendor.

Long feathers can establish the lines for an outstanding design. The brilliant colors blend with the camellia blooms and help solve the problem of height for short-stemmed flowers.

I have by no means exhausted the possibilities of creative design with camellias and accessories; I have merely suggested. For the designer who draws on his imagination and experience on the one hand, and on the wealth of objects of art, natural and man-made, on the other, the range of designs is virtually infinite.

Plate 67   *I often change the camellias in my arrangements, but here I have changed only the dominant line. The clipped palmetto palm gives a much bolder and more modern note to the design than the hydrangeas in the preceding illustration.*

Plate 68 *Containers need not be expensive to be handsome.*
This quite inexpensive one of black pottery was made within a
few miles of my home. The black bridge base is a compatible
choice and emphasizes the stark lines of the container. For this
Japanese Nageire arrangement, I chose two dramatic clipped
pine branches and a bloom and bud of beautiful Magnoliaeflora
camellia. Two sticks were wedged near the top of the container
in the form of a cross to support the branches and hold them at
the desired angle, and the camellias were then easily balanced
within the design.

CONTAINERS

The container is more than a vessel to hold flowers and water; it is an integral part of the design. Select them with good structural lines and an affinity for the flowers as well as the rooms where they are to be used. Strong simple containers having a look of stability suit the bold camellias; delicate containers are fine for small blossoms.

"Cute" containers, such as the glazed animal characters sold in many shops, are amusing but floral art is better served when a container has lovely lines, is neutral in color, and does not impose its own form on the beholder.

This does not mean that all containers must be expensive. Many low-priced containers of pottery, metal, glass and synthetic materials are on the market. Because they are understated, they are effective and easy to use, but their only purpose is to hold plant material; otherwise, they should be stored.

In a special group are the richly-decorated containers which are themselves works of art. The more highly ornamented they are, the more difficult the problem of designing flowers to fit. For the sake of unity, containers of this type usually should dominate the flowers. If the container has a painted design, repeat the color and form of the design with flowers. Not all antiques are a problem, however. Many are so neutral and subdued in feeling that a wide range of designs may be realized in them. The rare celadon vase shown in Color Plate VI is an example.

BASES AND STANDS

Bases serve in a number of ways: they improve the proportions of an arrangement by extending its dimensions so that it fully complements and beautifies a given space; improve the balance and impart stability to the design, particularly a tall, slender one or a top-heavy one; create a feeling of unity when accessories are used; give a finished look to a composition; protect surfaces against water damage and scratches; add distinction and style. Bases are often decorative in themselves and can add importance to a simple design.

Like containers, they come in all sizes, from small ones to be placed on end tables to those large enough to stand on the floor by themselves. They may range from exquisite old oriental stands to plain blocks of wood, rocks, or slate. Bases and stands should be simple of line and related in shape and character to the vases and flowers. They are a part of the total design; keep them well-groomed and free from water marks.

Plate 69   *To avoid top-heaviness, a replica of a Mexican museum piece is placed on a large base. It holds branches of clipped pine, ti leaves and ginger blooms from my Mother's garden in Florida, and a camellia seedpod. The Japanese consider the seed pod, or nut, of the camellia tree more important than the blossoms because they are the essence of life. Seeds which we are not planning to plant give interest and distinction to flower arrangements. I particularly like them in designs with fruit.*

Plate 70   *A grey root from a mountain lake fits in the neck of the grey pottery
container with no contrived mechanics. One camellia, any variety, completes the
arrangement which is placed on a beautiful old hand-carved stand. The arrangement was used in a lecture-demonstration for the Southeastern Regional Garden
Club Meeting one spring. Later, my daughter confiscated the container and driftwood and used it for months on an antique chest without ever tiring of it. Other
flowers were substituted for camellias when necessary—but that's another book!*

Plate 71 *The purple-pink of Martha Brice camellias, the blue of the modern Japanese flower container, and the green of the sago palm made a pleasing color combination for this arrangement made for a lecture-demonstration for the Garden Club of North Carolina state convention. The Japanese bridge added to the distinction of the design.*

Plate 72   *Edgeworthia from Japan was sprayed with flat black paint and impaled on a needlepoint holder in a black modern cylinder. One rubber plant leaf, one Blood of China camellia and one stalk of red gladiolus the exact shade of the camellia give dramatic impact to this modern arrangement made for a lecture-demonstration.*

Plate 73   *Roadside weeds impaled in a hidden pincup frame a serenely beautiful Mexican carved figure which dominates the composition, with September Morn camellias used as accessories. The figure stands on my desk when not used with flowers as a pleasant reminder of far places.*

Plate 74   *This rhythmic, swirling cypress root, exposed by hurricane Donna, was found on a fishing trip. Here it is used with a bold Lady Clare camellia and a large philodendron leaf in a modern white Japanese container on a black lacquer base edged in the red of the camellia. Our fishing guide is probably still shaking his head over a man who allows his wife to gather useless water-tumbled roots when the fish are biting!*

Plate 75   *The dead pine branch I picked up during a walk in the woods had lovely lines that required no pruning, and fitted into the tall celadon container with no mechancis other than one small stick inserted crosswise near the top of the vase. A piece of live pine and White Empress camellias completed the arrangement and made it suitable for many places in a home where a tall arrangement is needed.*

Plate 76   *A rough-textured stone conceals a large pincup holder on which the gnarled pine branch is impaled. Bits of fern, moss, and partially opened sasanqua blooms give a woodsy atmosphere and the feeling that the pine branch is a bonsai. The container is beige pottery, the base, a large bamboo mat.*

Plate 77   *A free-standing piece of driftwood bleached by sun and sand is given the importance of sculpture. White Queen camellias placed in orchid tubes and taped to the wood completed a pleasing arrangement for a picnic table.*

Plate 78 *A columnar black container furnishes an excellent foil for an often-used white figure handled here in an unusual way. White Florence Stratton camellias carry the eye from the sculpture to the rhythmic roots which we found on a lake shore. Miniature pine is used for filler. The design is anchored in water-filled Oasis cut to fit the neck of the container.*

$\mathcal{T}$OOLS AND TECHNIQUES

The tools and techniques of the trade are the crux of good flower arrangements. They can be elaborate or basic, but they must be adequate for their function, which is to impose a lasting design pattern on the organic materials of our medium.

PINHOLDERS

For most holding purposes I rely on a pinholder. Select one as heavy as possible, with the needles close together, and as large as your container will permit. The larger the holder, the less likely you are to run out of needles when you are working on a design with lots of flowers.

You will have to keep the holder from slipping around in the container. If the arrangement is not to be moved and the material to be arranged is light, place a small piece of paper towelling or newspaper, or a leaf, under the holder.

If the arrangement is to be carried a distance, or if the plant material is heavy, first anchor the holder to the container. To do this, roll a strip of floral clay about ¼″ wide and as long as necessary to girdle the outer edge of the holder. Press the clay

Plate 79   A flared pincup fits snugly into the top of the container which makes insertion of plant material easy, and avoids
possible scratching of the valuable container. Graceful leaves of
pineapple plant, umbrella palms and one Eleanor Hagood camellia with bud are arranged in an ancient oriental bronze vase
on an old burl, placed on a small living-room table.

lightly onto the bottom of the holder, then press the holder into the container (needles facing up, of course) making a slight twisting motion. There it is—a well-secured holder. Only one caution, be sure holder and container are dry or the clay won't stick.

FOR TALL CONTAINERS

I use several techniques for very tall vases. Sometimes I fill inexpensive ones to within a few inches from the top with sand, bird gravel, peat moss, or crushed wet newspaper from which most of the water is pressed out. On top of this I place some dry material, then add the pinholder, anchored with floral clay or held with melted paraffin. In the latter case, first melt the paraffin (old candles work well too) in a can or pot over the stove. Then pour a layer of the hot wax about ⅛″ thick (not enough to get to the needles) into the container, over the built-up sand or whatever material you used for the stuffing. Finally, lower the holder gently into the hot wax, knowing that it will be secure enough for very heavy material. While this method is quite satisfactory, it is not recommended for expensive containers.

The Japanese, since their ways with flowers are centuries old, have had plenty of time to develop fine methods, some of them appealing strongly to one's sense of economy. The most useful method is this one: Cut two twigs or branches of the right size to be wedged firmly into the neck of the container in the form of a cross, and they will support the flowers and branches easily.

Often a cup needlepoint holder can be found that is perfectly sized for the top of tall containers flared at the top. It is also functional when you are using a valuable container which you might hesitate to stuff. The cup holder even makes it possible for you to dispense with any vase at all, since the necessary needles are built into it, as is a well for water to keep the flowers fresh. Plate 79 and many other arrangements in the book are done in this way. Conceal the holder with large leaves, pieces of moss, rocks or whatever your inventiveness and sense of fitness suggest.

Oasis, which can be secured from your florist, can be wedged into a tall container to serve as holder for your flowers. First soak it for about an hour in water.

CONCEALING THE MECHANICS

If you are making an arrangement in a shallow glass container which is seen from above—for a low table, for instance—you can first wrap the pinholder in white tissue paper. For a silver tray, wrap the holder in aluminum foil.

Pebbles, rocks, chips of glass, weathered wood, moss, large leaves, or clusters of small ones . . . there is no end to the possibilities; they are only limited by your imagination!

TECHNIQUES WITH STEMS AND PETALS

Hollow stems from flowers or branches—gladiolas, for example —are useful for holding flowers, fruits or vegetables whose own stems are too short, thin or fragile to be placed directly into the holder. Fasten together the hollow stem and the plant material which it supports. Sometimes the flower stem will slip into the improvised stem. If the hollow stem is not rigid enough, reinforce it with a thin stick.
reinforce it with a thin stick.

I also use a plastic flower vial which is on the market. One end of the vial has a slit into which the short-stemmed flower is placed; the other end of the vial slips snugly over the florist stick, or a stick of your own contrivance.

In England in the nineteenth century, *The British Florist*, in discussing camellias, made this statement, "the blossoms are of a firm texture, but apt to fall off long before they have lost their brilliancy; it, therefore, is a practice with some to stick such deciduous blossoms on some fresh bud, where they continue to look well for a considerable time."

To solve the problem of flower-dropping, run a small wire through the calyx and twist it around the stem so that it is not visible. Generally, the single varieties drop much more quickly than the very double ones.

Plate 80   *Two pruned mahonia branches were wired to one end of a straight stick. The free end of the stick rests on the bottom of the container, and the base of the mahonia rests against the side of the container. Once the main branches were in place, it was easy to balance the pine and High Hat camellias in the design.*

Plate 81 *You'll need the sturdy clippers for pine branches! A tall pewter container on a burl holds Dr. Tinsley camellias and pine held in place with two crossed sticks at the opening. The camellias are then balanced within the design. Such an arrangement can be enjoyed for weeks by removing the camellias and replacing them as they fade. I made this for my husband's office.*

OTHER EQUIPMENT

A sharp pair of sturdy clippers is an absolute essential. So too is a fine water spray or syringe for creating the mist which camellia blooms like; also florist wire in several gages (gage 24 is the most all-purpose one) and florist sticks. Green floral tape is useful and so is a roll of cellophane tape. Soon you will have your own ideas about equipment too. Now put everything in a box or basket where it will be handy and have fun!

CUTTING, CONDITIONING AND GROOMING PLANT MATERIAL

1. Cut the flowers (see section on pruning for details) when they are turgid—early in the morning or, second choice, late in the afternoon. A large flat tray is ideal to carry to the garden to hold the cut blossoms.
2. If flowers are picked on a warm, dry day, make them turgid and of good substance by spraying with a fine mist of water and placing in the refrigerator overnight under high humidity. High humidity first, and proper refrigeration second, are important factors in keeping camellias. They are extremely sensitive to humidity levels. They take and lose moisture readily through their petals and require frequent misting for long life. Flowers which have become limp or wilted often can be made crisp by the same treatment, providing they are not bruised. Always handle camellia blooms *gently*. No amount of conditioning can restore a flower that has been bruised or crushed by careless handling.
3. The experienced arranger usually takes flowers of different sizes, including a few partly open flowers and buds. Most camellia blooms do not develop or open further after cutting, so cut them at the stage of development desired. Do not cut old flowers; their colors are faded and they soon fall from the stem.
4. Remove all bruised leaves and flowers. With a small scissors snip off insect damage and undesirable leaves. Branches or twigs that confuse the design should be trimmed out or bent to more desirable positions.
5. To clean camellia and similar foliage, rinse and wipe care-

fully, or if it is very dirty, wash in lukewarm, soapy water. If more sheen is desired, polish leaves with crumpled green wax paper such as florists use: but beware of over-grooming. Never grease or make foliage look artificial.

6. It is seldom that a branch curves exactly as the arranger wants, so as to appear to be growing gracefully from the container. You can manipulate it to achieve the desired effect. To bend a branch, take care not to put too much force in a concentrated area lest it snap. Holding it in both hands, placed close together, gently bend and twist branch simultaneously. Sometimes several curves are necessary to achieve the desired line.

7. To condition foliage from the garden, immerse in water for several hours or overnight. Camellia foliage has superb keeping qualities and can be kept fresh and usable for weeks. Be sure to strip leaves from that part of the stem which will be under water, so they will not decay and foul the water.

8. Recut stems under water at time of arranging. Florist flowers should be cut, and the flowers plunged into water, set in a cool place for several hours or until ready to arrange.

Thick branches should be cut on a slant and then recut diagonally, making a sharper point (to fit more easily into holder). They may also be split a number of times or crushed at the end in order that they can be more securely impaled. This will also increase their intake of water.

TIPS FOR THE NEW ARRANGER

1. Secure the holder to the container—centered if you are making a symmetrical arrangement, off center for an asymmetrical one.

2. Select and insert the longest or main branch in the holder. Tilt it to the desired direction. The other lines are then easier to choose and place. If you don't know how long a branch to use, try it one and one-half to two times longer than the container.

3. Don't use too many different flowers unless you are aiming

Plate 82 *A long grey cascading root hooks easily and fits snugly over the rim of the tall pewter container. Natural openings hold short pine branches, and Casablanca and Bryan Wright camellias. The arrangement was used on a long low table.*

Plate 83 *To avoid guesswork, compose the arrangement at the place it is to decorate. Forced green tips of gum tree were shortened when they seemed too tall for the small table. Curled aspidistra leaves and Rose Dawn camellias complete an early-spring arrangement in a needlepoint holder concealed with grey moss.*

for a period-bouquet look. Let every branch or bloom *count;* don't make meaningless additions. Undercrowded arrangements look better—and keep better.

4. When the arrangement is "on location", look at it impersonally and critically (this is hard; enthusiasm for one's own efforts gets in the way). Then view it as others will and on the same eye level—sit at the table (test from all sides) to view a centerpiece, on the sofa to check the design for the coffee table. Analyze and learn from your mistakes.

5. Spray the finished arrangement with a fine water spray to increase the life span of camellias, and other flowers too. Change water in arrangements daily. Clean water and fresh, cool air are the best preservatives for any flower.

Nothing is lovelier, I think, than sun rays playing on translucent petals, but drafts, heat and sun do shorten the life of arrangements.

STORING BLOOMS

Camellia blooms can be kept beautiful and usable for two or more weeks if properly stored. They should be placed in an airtight box lined with shredded wax paper, soft tissue or moss. Sprinkle or spray blooms with fine mist and set in a dark, cold place. There are very fine aluminum boxes made especially for storing and transporting camellia blooms. However, an ordinary pasteboard box may be made airtight by the use of foil or Saran wrap. Plastic refrigerator boxes with covers are excellent for storing camellias also.

Coating flowers to reduce water loss, or treating them with synthetic hormones and nutrient solutions have increased their life in some instances. The Japanese use plain table salt to prolong the life of camellia blooms. They allow camellia stems to stand for one hour in cold water to which a pinch of salt has been added, and sprinkle a strong brine into the blossom itself to delay browning of petals. Working salt into the base of the stamens with a small stick is recommended to prevent flowers from falling.

Plate 84 *The placement and economy of material in a con-*
temporary bronze Japanese usubata made it ideal and practical
on a contemporary chest against a dark panelled wall in my hus-
band's office. Stalks of red sugar cane impaled on a needlepoint
holder with one large philodendron leaf in opposition formed a
long-lasting background for a succession of camellia blooms.
Here it is shown with an Are-jishi camellia which is the exact
color of the sugar cane. The holder is covered with small pebbles.

Plate 85 *The upright Japanese design and Aztec container are admirably*
harmonious. Loquat with its bronzy under-leaf and bloom, and the brown
and black of the container on a slick black base, made an interesting color
and texture contrast against the beige walls of my study. The camellia is
Victory White. Gravel in the container raises the needlepoint holder to a
few inches from the top of the container for easy insertion of plant material.

CORSAGES

Through the ages man has used flowers to beautify his existence. Ancient Egyptian tomb paintings show flowers in the headdress of many of the figures. In classical Greece and Rome, flowers were worn as garlands in the hair and at the waist. In the Pacific, Polynesian women have long tucked flowers behind their ears and worn leis of flowers around the neck. In our time and country, corsages are worn for many occasions, and few brides or bridesmaids would dream of going to the altar without one!

Of all the flowers which are used, none is more lasting or more versatile than the camellia. In its wide range of type, form, size, and color, a perfect complement for any costume may be found.

There are many different ways to make corsages, but the method demonstrated to me many years ago by Mr. S. L. Marbury, President Emeritus of the American Camellia Society, has proved to be the simplest and most effective. By this technique, anyone can create corsages which equal those made by a fine florist. The following materials are required:

> Green florist wire heavy enough to push through the calyx; size 24 is strong enough for any flower.
>
> Green florist tape. Other colors may be used for special work, weddings, for example, but green is best generally.
>
> Cardboard collars. Known in the florist trade as gardenia collars. (They can be made out of light cardboard cut to the desired shape or size.)
>
> Scissors and a stapler.

To make the corsage, select a fresh, perfect bloom appropriate in size, form, texture, and color to the occasion or use. Gently twist the bloom from its stem. Holding the bloom firmly between thumb and forefinger of one hand, insert a ten-inch piece of wire straight through the base of the petals and calyx until centered, taking care that the wire does not penetrate any visible front petals. Insert a second piece of wire of the

Plate 86   *Flower-holder technique can be simple or extremely intricate. Here a piece of driftwood, picked up on a mountain lake shore, balanced easily on top of the modern pottery container. Camellias species C. Hiemalis, Shishi-Gashira are held by a small oblong needlepoint holder, permanently anchored in the container.*

same length in the same way but at right angles to the first; gently bend down four ends and twist together to form an artificial stem. Conceal wire stem with green floral tape, wrapped spirally (stretching tape slightly as you work). If gardenia collars are being used, twist two or three extra layers of tape close to the blossom to form a small knob that will slip through the collar and help hold the bloom firmly.

The corsage is now ready for leaves. They can be added in one of two ways. You can run a light wire through the base of a leaf, bending the wire down and twisting it around the artificial stem of the flower. Or, even better, if you have a florist gardenia collar, staple two or three leaves to it. After the leaves are attached to the collar, pass the wire stem of the camellia through the collar and snugly, but gently, pull the collar against the base of the bloom to lock into place. Tilt the flower head forward to the desired position. The artificial stem is curled around in any desired way. The flower is now ready to be worn. A single camellia with no embellishment can be glamorous.

For a corsage of several blooms, combine the individually prepared flowers into a pleasing group. Wire together or fit on a form from the florist.

Taste and occasion may dictate the use of other flowers with camellias. Bows, lace, net and other materials are often used, but restraint should be exercised for best effects.

Each garden should boast a miniature flowering camellia plant to supply boutonnieres for the man of the house. If no miniature is in bloom, select a small bud for this use.

A camellia corsage, properly made and carefully handled, can be worn again and again over a period of days. Do not bruise the flower. Lightly spray with water after each wearing. Place in a tightly covered box and keep in the refrigerator or other cool place.

Plate 87   A handsome container, hand-made in North Carolina, holds a root, one dried brown aspidistra leaf and one White Empress camellia. Plant material is wedged into the small opening of the container with a few small stems.

INDEX